Nine Famous Artists Your Children Will Love

An Art Discovery Primer & Handbook
for Parents and their Children

Michael Napoliello Jr.

Literary Press

Published by Literary Press
Newport Beach, California
800-339-0551
www.literarypress.com
In collaboration with the Pasadena Museum of California Art

Library of Congress Control No. 203104707
ISBN 0-9716958-4-9

Cover and interior design by Heather Buchman

Cover Art:
Upper left, Alexander Calder, ***Etching with Star, Boat and Waves***
Upper right, Joan Miró, 1948 illustration
Lower Left, Roy Lichtenstein, ***Reverie***
Lower right, David Smith, ***VB XXIII***

Proceeds from the sale of this book help to fund educational programs at the Pasadena Museum of California Art.

Dedication

For Shannon Harold, Cosette Moskowitz, Alexis and my many, and wonderful, Godsons.

Contents

Acknowledgments

It would take another book to note the help and inspiration of all the people that made this book possible. But it is hard to imagine getting this done without the support of the following…

The Des Moines Art Center is where the idea for this book was conceived. Their "uncommon vision" has created, despite the odds, a place that epitomizes what this book is about—a day with the family surrounded by wonderful art is more than art appreciation, it is life appreciation.

Shannon Harold always makes the most sacrifices for my work.

Robert Woodcox has been co-conspirator and coach since I started.

I would also like to thank Wesley Jessup and Nancy Silverman-Miles for their intellectual insights and cooperation with some of the nuts and bolts of getting this to print.

Introduction

You might think, having written this book, I had a calling. I call it more of a dragging. I remember, at about age ten, my parents dragged me to the National Gallery of Art in Washington, D.C. As we walked up the impossibly large entry steps, it was hard for my little legs and brain to imagine a worse fate.

But, the minute we walked in the Rotunda, my eyes were filled by a wonder no comic book hero could ever match: the larger than life marble sculpture of the god Mercury. When I asked my father why Mercury had wings on his feet and he told me they were to speed his many epic journeys, I was hooked. Hooked on an inspiration I could not explain at that tender age and hooked on my Dad. As you can imagine, it was a good day.

For the next thirty years, many people have asked me about my passion for art. Most questions in the "what's the big deal" vein. In general I say that the appreciation of art can provide insight and inspiration for all you do in life whether you are a lawyer, athlete, parent and/or all of the above. But if you had asked me and you were a parent, my answer would be a bit more specific and impassioned . . . perhaps going back to that wonderful day in D.C.

It is my contention that children who are exposed to art at an early age and who then grow up appreciating it, through a lifelong discovery, aided and abetted by their parents, end up being brighter, happier and healthier human beings. But don't take my word for it alone. You'll be amazed at what some of the experts have to say within these pages about your child's potential—especially if he or she begins to enjoy art with you.

There is just one last thing I want to say and then I'll let you begin your journey. Have fun for Heaven's sake!

— Michael Napoliello Jr.

Chapter One

WOW!

"The weekend's coming. What are we going to do with the kids?"

"The zoo?"

"They've been there twice."

"Disneyland?"

"Are you crazy? We spent a fortune the last time we went there."

"I've got it, Chuck E. Cheese!"

"You're no help at all."

Sound familiar? This conversation, or a variation, takes place every week in homes all over America. Just what is there to do with your children this weekend? Let's make a list. Assuming your children are between the ages of about six and twelve, there are: theme parks, the zoo, the circus (once a year), Chuck E. Cheese's (or places like that), a movie, the park, your backyard or the television. With the exception of the park and your own home, most of these other venues are not free. In fact, as you are probably already well aware, they can be quite expensive and besides, you've already been there and done that.

However, there is an alternative, a very good one, one that you might have overlooked.

What would you say if I told you there is a place, very near you, perhaps just around the corner, where you and your children can enjoy an afternoon that is: ***fun, exciting, stimulating, and very inexpensive?*** You would probably want to know what it is, wouldn't you? I'm going to tell you in a moment, but you have to promise me, you won't be intimidated and you won't just slam the cover of this book shut—it's an art museum.

I can hear the groans.

"Oh God," you're saying. "What is my child going to do in an art museum? He'd be bored to death if there weren't any dinosaurs there—so would I."

Perhaps the words "art gallery" would have been better because that's what this book is really all about, art that you and your children will love, and besides, you did promise to give me a little latitude. Before you give up on the idea entirely, allow me just a moment more of your time—I promise you won't be sorry.

Theme parks, movies, arcades and baseball games are all great for the kids, and they're certainly fun and entertaining, but after a while, even these activities can lose some of their excitement and, of course, there is always the cost factor. Art is different and, unlike some of these other choices, it's very inexpensive and accessible. Even a simple movie for a family of four can set you back close to $50 these days. Like movies, nearly every city in

America has a museum or art gallery and most are quite inexpensive. In many cases children under the age of twelve are free and adult tickets rarely cost more than $12. More importantly though, it can bring joy into your child's life, provide knowledge and set him or her on a lifelong path of discovery. Can you say that about a trip to Chuck E. Cheese's?

Parents have known for quite some time, and science has proven, that ***the experiences of the early years of childhood are the building blocks to all future intellectual growth.***

As you will soon read, the experts testify that learning begins as early as day one. The best parents are constantly looking for ways to give their children new and enlightening experiences, so much the better if they are fun. One of the richest treasure chests in terms of learning, and yet one that is probably the most underutilized, is the vast body of great works of art—just waiting for you and your child to enjoy them. However, for the purposes of this first volume, we will be exploring and enjoying nine specific artists.

There are many benefits that you may not be aware of that you and your child will derive from an involvement in art; I've chosen to break them into three categories:

- **Fun**
- **Parent/child dialogue**
- **Lifelong discovery and enhanced learning**

BENEFIT #1. FUN

First let's agree on one thing: the world of art can be frightening to most people. Fortunately, it's mostly the adults that are afraid. I also realize that museums can be forbidding structures. Some look like they were built for Roman emperors. Others are ultra modernistic, surrounded by weird sculptures that make no sense. If you do make it inside, it can be so quiet, it's downright intimidating, and at first it may seem that there is no one around to help you. In addition, the galleries can go on forever with no place to sit. And, "art experts" seem to be snobs; their attitude may be that art is only for the "highly educated." When asked for an opinion, the "experts" may not bother to answer you, or if they do, they might sound like a talking art history book.

So, what's the upside? Yes, museums can be confusing and the language of art can be intimidating, and sure, the art world has its snobs. However, in recent years museums have spent a great deal of time trying to become more hospitable and, unbelievably, more fun. Great exhibitions and friendlier employees are becoming the norm. As far as the curators or the experts go, if you show some enthusiasm in their field, most of them won't let you out of their sight.

Most importantly, you have this book and these wonderful, exciting and fun artists to explore on your own. And, don't forget, museums are very inexpensive and are quite accessible. If you look at a museum through the eyes of a child, you'll see that it's really just one giant visual playground. Besides, this book isn't just about museums, though it does offer some valuable insights on how to visit one; it's about the artists and having some fun.

Learning through play

As we become adults, we have a tendency to stop playing. We sometimes also lose our ability to get excited about discovering new things, and we lose our eagerness to learn, all of which I find very sad.

Do you remember when you were a child and you could play with toys for hours on end and be oblivious to everything around you? You may not remember, but you were lost in what you were doing. That is the true essence of play. The very first things we played with as babies were colorful shapes. This could have been a mobile hanging overhead in the crib or a simple plastic toy. Colorful visual things were usually our first stimulus after noise. Even as we just "played" at those early ages from birth to about three, we were learning, despite ourselves. We were looking, listening and touching everything around us. Babies discover by seeing, reaching and touching. At each stage of our development, we discovered the world around us in this manner.

Introducing art to your child is another way to enhance his or her sense of discovery and for him or her to learn and to have fun at the same time.

Technically speaking, you, the parent, are your child's first big toy. For the most part, your child likes what you like, so the more you know about art yourself, the more your child will learn, and you'll both have great fun interacting with each other over what you discover.

In her book, ***Toy's Smart Play,*** author Stevanne Auerbach, Ph.D., says with respect to play, "A playful parent encourages a child to be playful and a more playful child is more aware, smarter and more resilient. The benefits to the whole family are enormous. And do I need to mention how your whole relationship with your child will be strengthened?"

Becoming involved with art is play. Playing is a form of discovery and discovery is learning, all of which is quite fun.

Dr. Auerbach goes on to point out the advantages of play experiences, which include:

- *Gaining an understanding of the world*
- *Enhancing the ability to concentrate, an essential skill before he or she even begins school*
- *Expanding natural curiosity, whets his appetite to solve problems and fosters spontaneity, all of which are central components of mastering the learning process*

Okay, so you're still having a little problem equating art and fun. So how exactly is art fun you ask? Good question. Remember the colorful plastic mobile we talked about a minute ago, the one that hung over your head as you fidgeted in your crib? That toy was inspired in miniature, by a gentleman who was enthralled with an Alexander Calder mobile, one of the artists in this book.

The fun of experiencing and understanding art can stimulate the senses as well as the intellect of your child. In fact, it can be downright joyous. This weekend ask your son if he would like to go see giant, shiny, metallic robots, and then enjoy watching his face light up. Or, ask your daughter if she would like to visit an enormous upside down flower garden that moves and turns with no motors or strings. My guess is that in either case the reaction will be a hearty and enthusiastic yes! And when the two of you finally do experience these works, when you smile and laugh together and you have a lively discourse about what you are seeing or touching, then you will know how and why art is fun.

One of the reasons I've chosen these nine artists is because they were all quite playful people themselves and their art is just plain fun to look at and to touch. I also chose these "modern" artists, or expressionists because their art represents a time when artists "allowed" themselves to go far beyond the restricted practice of copying a subject faithfully. With this generation, pure energy was being expressed for the first time in the history of art, and with it the mysteries of emotion.

Here are some snapshots of the artists you will come to know:

Alexander Calder was a sculptor who perfected the art of creating giant, brightly colored mobiles; I call them "toys for geniuses." When he was young, he was obsessed with the circus and would create figures like clowns and animals and use them to put on shows in his room. Your child will be tickled to see his enormous shapes twist and turn with no apparent wind to blow them. Think of the discussions that will stimulate.

Red Grooms was a painter and sculptor. He loved staging live "happenings" that were a cross between a play and a piece of art (we will talk about these later). He also created playful and unique constructions of famous people using cardboard and paper. His very unusual art has a marvelous sense of humor and irony that children instinctively love.

Claes Oldenburg, a painter and sculptor, is famous for taking common everyday items and turning them into extraordinary visual experiences. Try to visualize a twenty-foot tall ice cream cone made from soft vinyl stuffed with tons of beanbag material, one of his most famous works. What child could keep his or her hands off that? When the city of New York asked him for ideas to create a monument in Central Park, he suggested he make a giant teddy bear more than fifty feet in height. Unfortunately, they never took him up on it.

Roy Lichtenstein was famous for his inventive use of a material called "Benday" that is used in the printing of comic books. In fact, most of his art is just that, giant cartoons. Ask your child this weekend if she would like to go see a ten-foot high comic strip, or a huge poster of Mickey Mouse and watch her face light up.

Joan Miró, a painter and sculptor, believed that children's drawings were the essence of all that was good. They were honest, creative, fun and simple. As with many of the artists in this book, your child is likely to look at his work and say, "I can do that." One of his most memorable works was a mobile entitled ***Harlequin's Carnival,*** which is made up of giant insects dancing and playing music.

Jackson Pollock, perhaps the most famous of this group, would probably inspire you and your child, more than the others would, to ask, "What was he thinking?" Now that he has been the subject of a popular movie, you may be familiar with his "drip" paintings. After years of experimenting with surrealism, cubism and other forms of art that might be considered to have "deeper meanings," Pollock discovered the sheer joy of splattering, spilling, dripping and flicking paint onto a canvas—what could be more childlike and fun? Most children will relate their adventures with finger painting when viewing Pollock.

Wassily Kandinsky's work was similar to Miró's. Kandinsky will surely stimulate your child's imagination. He was also an accomplished musician who once said,

> *Color is the keyboard, the eyes are the harmonies, the soul is the piano with many strings. The artist is the hand that plays, touching one key or another to cause vibrations in the soul.*

Think about the impression that art can make on a child the next time you view a Kandinsky. Think about this: he gave up a career as a college professor primarily because of the powerful impression that a *single painting* made on him, a Monet entitled ***Haystack*** (see artists' biographies). What fire could a trip to the museum light under your child.

Fernand Léger may be the least known of these nine Famous Artists but his scenes of everyday life, that look like busy circus posters, are fascinating in their detail. Your child could literally spend an hour discovering the minute and colorful people, objects and activities that populate his paintings. You'll have as much fun as your children asking them to identify as many characters as possible.

David Smith is what I call "a magician with metal." He is best known for his giant, shiny, metallic robot-like beings called ***Cubis,*** among other metal sculptures. What child isn't fascinated with magic, or robots for that matter?

BENEFIT #2. PARENT/CHILD DIALOGUE

In this day and age, when parents compete with video games, television and the Internet for their child's attention, what could be more important than creating an open dialogue?

Communicating with your child is one of modern life's real challenges (come to think of it, communicating with anyone can be a challenge), but if you can keep the channels open you can dramatically change his attitudes, self-image, rate of learning and the degree to which he learns.

I recently watched a good anti-drug, public service announcement on television. The whole point of the spot was to remind parents to ask their children, "Where are you going? Who were you with? What were you doing?" The only question that was missing (and probably the most important) was, "What are you thinking?" The importance of talking and listening to your children cannot be overstated.

Experiencing art together has the power to open channels of communication between you and your children. As we all know, children are naturally curious, asking questions that confound us, "Mommy, why doesn't it rain up? Daddy, where does the sun go when it gets dark? Why does my hamster pee when I tickle his belly?" Can you imagine the questions your children will ask when you take them to see Claes Oldenburg's giant ice cream cone? By becoming more knowledgeable yourself with these nine artists, you will be able to answer some of those questions and you will begin to ask some interesting ones yourself, ideas and thoughts that you can share with your child.

> *A "grown up" dialogue is a wondrous thing for a child. Conversations with adults usually come in the "I'm the teacher, you're the student" variety. Discussing art and enjoying it together (adult dialogue) creates equality and gives your child stature. Art is a neutral ground for both of you and it might be the first conversation where the child is equal with his parent. This strengthens the child's self esteem.*

BENEFIT #3. LIFELONG DISCOVERY AND ENHANCED LEARNING

According to Joan Beck in her best selling book, ***How To Raise A Brighter Child,*** "Cognitive learning begins as early as three years of age." She says, "You, the parent, are the first and the best teachers. You have the unique opportunity to boost your child's intelligence when it is most subject to change, to teach him or her individually, at his own pace and when, and by what means, he is most likely to learn to shape your relationship with him in ways that can actually help him become brighter."

Certainly it's fun and important to spend time with your child in a variety of ways: going to the movies, watching their soccer matches, Disneyland, but wouldn't it be great if they could have just as much fun, spending quality time with you, and learn something all in one convenient and inexpensive place?

I think we can agree on one thing before we go any further: children are born with a certain amount of innate intelligence and creativity; the rest is learned. Further, as Joan Beck's book proves, ***you*** can raise a brighter, more creative child and bright, creative children grow into bright and creative adults. And—I'll really go out on a limb here and say—happier, healthier and emotionally well-balanced adults as well.

Enhanced learning
Raising brighter, happier children

There are two generally supported theories of learning: the behavioral approach, and the cognitive approach. The word "cognitive'" refers to learning in the broadest sense. This involves complex mental processes including memory, attention, language, concept formation and problem solving. ***The study and enjoyment of art exercises all of these processes.*** To experience the shapes, colors and textures of things is to be more in touch with the world, to be more alive, more open, and more resistant to stasis.

In the case of visual art, as opposed to music or writing, the learning process obviously involves observation. In observing art and learning more about it, we nurture the overall thinking, and the sense-making processes.

Both children and adults learn a great deal through observation and imitation. In a later chapter, we have provided you with "art projects," or "idea starters" you and your children can have fun with together. It is said that one of the most important ways we learn is through imitation. These aren't projects that copy the artist's work though; they are opportunities for your children to be creative and to have fun using the same materials and processes that the artists used in their works.

Words don't always convey some of our human perceptions and emotions, so art is essential to providing another means of discourse, a non-verbal means—the earlier, the better.

According to Joan Beck in ***How to Raise a Brighter Child***,

> *Even neuroscientists have been astounded to learn how rapidly a baby's brain grows, how literally trillions of neural connections form in the first few months of life, and how those connections disappear forever by about age ten, if they are not used. The brain, in effect, becomes hard-wired at an early age, and the learning opportunities a child has during those first few years can make a permanent difference in her lifelong level of intelligence.*

I bring this up because I feel it's better to start earlier than later to bring your child in contact with the appropriate stimulation, in our case, visual art, to allow your child to develop to his or her full potential. Until recently, even knowing scientists greatly underestimated what children under the age of six could and should be learning.

A child's ability to acquire many skills is dependent upon the amount and kind of stimulation and the opportunities afforded that child in his environment. In fact, some kinds of brain development may actually be ***dependent*** upon a child having certain kinds of environmental stimulation. Certainly, the joy of color, shapes and textures is one of these stimuli and it begins in the cradle when we hang colorful plastic shapes over their heads—mobiles.

Regardless of how, what, when, or where you teach your child, whether that's reading to him, using flashcards, playing music, or helping him review his multiplication tables, your role should also be that of a scene setter who provides an atmosphere of experiences in which you can share the exhilaration of learning. And of course, I feel the "atmosphere" of art is a vital ingredient in a child's learning growth. A life filled with discovery, begins with discovery.

Creative skills

Involving your children in art not only stimulates their curiosity, it opens channels of communication, it feeds their thirst for knowledge, and it can inspire them to great creative heights of their own.

It is important to reiterate here that **this is *not* a book about training your children to become future artists,** though there are worse things that could happen. **It *is* about setting the wheels in motion for a life filled with discovery, and having lots of fun along the way.**

Being creative means much more than having a talent for music or painting. **It involves adventurous thinking no matter what the field of endeavor**. It is the ability to originate your own unique new ideas, to see unexpected relationships, to formulate concepts rather than to learn by rote alone. The more creativity you encourage in your children, the more successful they will be later in life in whatever endeavors they choose whether that's art, science, politics, entertainment, sales or any other profession. I cannot stress this last statement enough.

Most people who consider themselves "fulfilled, happy and successful," also consider themselves creative thinkers, and indeed that is most often true.

At the lowest level, creative learning is just the simple thrill in seeing that when blue and yellow paint is mixed together, it turns to green. At the highest level there resides the solutions for a New World, and never has there been more need for a creative approach to the problems in our homes, communities, the nation and the world, than right now.

> *Art is simply a question of doing things, anything, well. When the artist is alive in any person, whatever his kind of work may be, he becomes an inventive, searching, daring, self-expressive creature. He finds gain in the work itself, not outside of it.*
>
> — Robert Henri

According to Joan Beck, "A creative child has intelligence of the highest order. But, that doesn't necessarily mean that he or she will score high on an IQ test, which measures chiefly academic areas of mental abilities.

"Most researchers agree on three things:

1) ***Almost all small children possess a considerable amount of creativity.***
2) ***Creativity can be increased by deliberate encouragement, opportunity and training.***
3) ***Creativity can also be dulled, almost out of existence, by some child-rearing practices."***

Creative children generate ideas like a hot pan of popcorn going off. Many of their ideas are offbeat, but some are also quite original. They often give unusual answers to questions and suggest unique solutions to problems. In chapter five when we discuss a visit to the art museum, I have given you what I call "dialogue starters." You can use these suggestions, and your own, of course, while viewing various pieces of art, to discover just how "offbeat and original" your child can be. Questions like, "Can you tell me a story about what you see? Or, "Does this picture remind you of anything?" The answers not only inspire an adult dialogue, they can be hilarious, sad, compelling, stimulating and entertaining.

What are the signs of creativity that you can watch for in your small child? Once again, Ms. Beck says, "Several researchers have compiled descriptions of creative children you'll find useful. For example, an enormous bump of curiosity is typical of creative youngster—he loves to experiment, to test the limits of situations. He questions constantly and usually in a penetrating way.

"A creative youngster is particularly sensitive to what he **sees, hears, touches and experiences.** You will notice this sensitivity in the pictures he draws or finger-paints, also in his surprising understanding of other people and other people's problems. He delights in learning precisely the right word for an object, or a feeling, or a color and he enjoys sharing these special observations with an adult who is also aware of them."

Reading what Beck has written, can there be any doubt that encouraging your child to experience art and opening a dialogue with her will cause her creative skills to blossom?

Your child may not grow up to be an artist, and that is all fine and well. The point is that no matter what he eventually becomes, if you have provided him these experiences and he becomes a more creative individual, he will most likely become more successful in any arena whether that is sports, medicine, the law or any other endeavor.

Just as a note: if your child did want to put his or her knowledge of art to work, without becoming an "artist," there are professions that work within and on the periphery of the arts that can provide your child with a satisfying and lucrative career such as a museum curator or museum administrator. Gallery event planners and marketing or public relations professionals also earn good salaries.

Not only are these professions lucrative but also there isn't the competition for these jobs that there are for many others. And just think, your child would also be doing something good for the world.

In addition to career opportunities, an early and lifelong appreciation for, and understanding of art, provides the background and knowledge that individuals need in developing their social skills, e.g., conversation and other interpersonal skills. A grounding in art can provide your child with the kind of insights in later life that can stimulate and inspire others and cause them to view your child in a wider perspective. Art also has a moral impact on those who enjoy it throughout their lives, helping them to discern what is tasteful and what isn't—what is important and what isn't.

Also, people who have grown up enjoying and learning about art find that as they become adults and begin to travel, galleries throughout the world offer an exciting and stimulating perspective on their individual societies and environments. A gallery is a great place to enjoy the day, be inspired, find resources and if nothing else, just a quiet place to enjoy a sandwich and meet interesting people.

Chapter Two

Why These Nine Artists?

Perhaps more than any other portion of this book, this chapter will help you understand the rewards that are waiting for you and your child through the enjoyment of, and involvement in, art.

When I set out to write this book, having studied art nearly all my life, I knew I was faced with the monumental task of choosing just the right artists to include. After all, there are thousands, and many of them would not be appropriate.

Foremost, the artists and their work had to be fun, engaging and provide the first step in a lifelong discovery. However, I realized that I had to be more specific, and so I began my selection process by coming up with what I called "filters." I applied two filters for the parents and four for the children. For the parents and the children alike, I decided that the ***content*** of the art should *not* be objectionable. Many great pieces of art deal with political and social issues that are not the best introduction for children. I felt that it was more important to have fun during the first steps.

Next, for the parents, I felt that the artists should be ***important,*** meaning they should all be well established, internationally known and respected, in the sense that they would be the door to future appreciation of all forms of art.

The filters for the children were even more important in that this could be their first and last exposure to art, depending upon the experience. Therefore, ***style, content, format*** and the ***tactile*** aspects of the art itself were important considerations.

In terms of style, I wanted to include art that was dynamic and colorful. For content, I chose expressionists, rather than conceptual artists. Expressionism is based more on the artist's emotions, while conceptual art is more concerned with ideas.

Format was an important concern for many reasons. I wanted to explore artists who were known for large, accessible works. Too many times, when a child is first taken to a museum or art gallery, the art is too small or too far away for children to relate to. Paintings are hung behind ropes, or high on walls, under strict security rules. We are not allowed to touch or to get too close to them. I wanted to explore art that children could experience up close physically.

My last criteria was that some of the art should ***do something***—move, make noise, or at least be art that a child could touch.

FILTERS FOR PARENTS:

- Content (non-objectionable)
- Importance

FILTERS FOR CHILDREN:

- Content (non-objectionable)
- Style
- Format
- Appearance
- Do something

Having prefaced my selection process, I began to slowly select the artists one at a time for inclusion into this book.

Here are some of the reasons I've included each and some of the reasons you and your children will be fascinated and entertained as well as enlightened through the enjoyment of their work:

ALEXANDER CALDER

Content: Circus animals, performers, flowers, and organic abstract shapes.

Importance: Perfected the mobile and stabile

Style, format, appearance: Childlike, playful, three-dimensional, large and easily viewed. Interactive nature. Vivid colors.

Do something: You can actually make them move by blowing on them, which in turn presents a completely different look to the art. My father taught me about ocean waves and how birds fly through Calder's art. It's more fun than blowing out the candles on a birthday cake!

Eleven Polychrome

Abstract Etching with Star and Serpent

RED GROOMS

Content: The poet, Lawrence Ferlenghetti, titled his most famous book *A Coney Island of the Mind.* He could have been writing about Groom's work—most often, sculptural pieces that invite one to invoke Disneyland or a Broadway comedy in their minds. In Grooms' art you will find farmers, businessmen, circus clowns and Moms ready for the supermarket, all presented with irrepressible humor, sympathy and hope for humanity.

Importance: A pioneer of pop art (short for popular art). He collaborated with another of our artists, Claes Oldenburg, and represented America in the 1996 Venice Biennale, the world's most prestigious modern art exhibition.

Style, format, appearance: Life-size and lifelike pieces depicting farm life, fantasy, cities and circuses that are fun and serious at the same time.

Do something: Take a walk around or inside one of Groom's pieces. The fun and fascination never ends.

Agricultural building

WASSILY KANDINSKY

Content: Vivid colors and textures. Abstracts. No objectionable content.

Importance: Was the first artist to step away from realism and to experiment with abstract pictures. He thought of color as music.

Style, format, appearance: Lively, colorful and large. Could view standing on your head and have as much fun as on your feet.

Do something: Look closely to find common, everyday images in the playful abstract backgrounds.

Improvisational painting

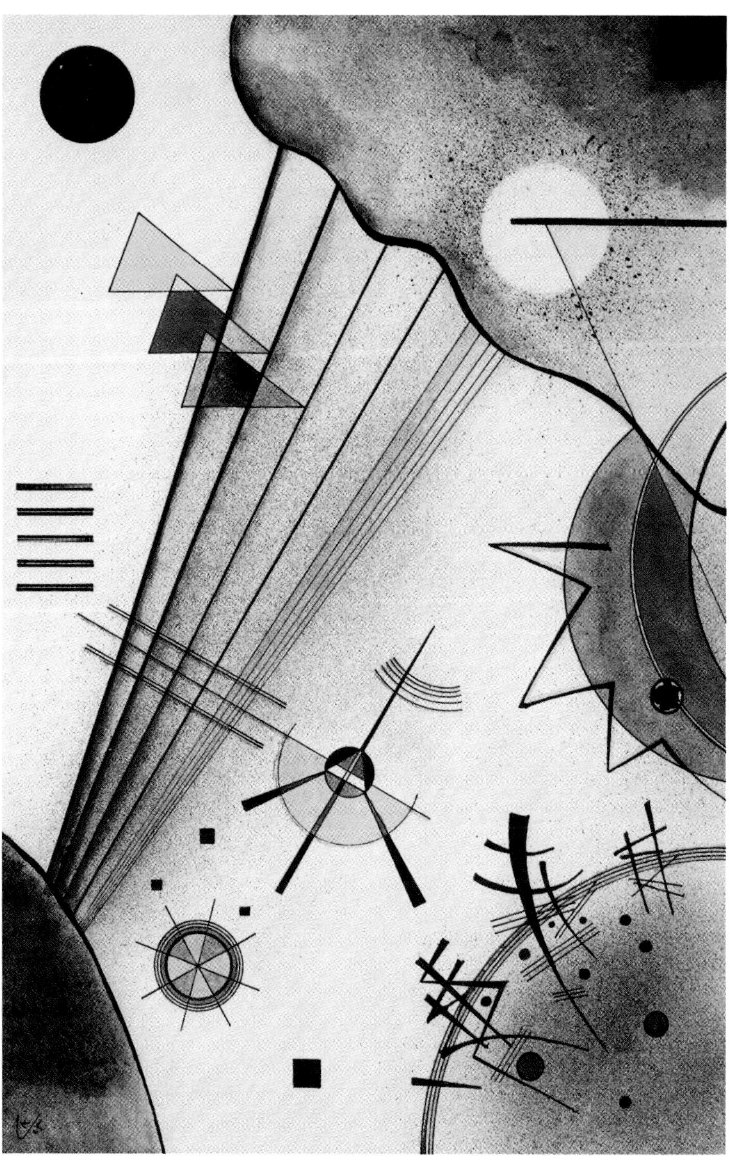

Clear Connection

ROY LICHTENSTEIN

Content: Cartoons. Amazing wit and imagination. Vivid colors. No objectionable content. Images often contain a white dialogue "balloon" that says things to the viewers. Fun, fun, fun!

Importance: One of the best-known artists of the 20th century. Was instrumental in the 1960s in the pop op movement.

Style, format, appearance: Kid friendly cartoons with lots of action and color. Most works are very large and are easily viewed at a distance or up close, depending upon how they are displayed.

Do something: Walk up close, very close and see the dots that comprise his images. Walk back, way back, and see how they seem to blend into nearly seamless images. Discover the Benday, cartoon-making process. In either case, the art does something quite different.

Varoom!

Reverie

FERNAND LÉGER

Content: This French master is best known for his paintings of stylized factories and the modern mechanized world done with a rich, almost cartoon-like quality. In his work, you can see the beauty, intensity and often fantasy-like complexity of the mechanized world. His work is a surrealistic adventure through our technological era as well as a bittersweet homage.

Importance: He was a contemporary of Picasso. Léger's popularity, based on his accessible themes, spread rapidly throughout the world. He is also one of the world's preeminent muralists whose works adorn many prominent buildings including the assembly hall of the UNESCO building in New York.

Style, format, appearance: Primarily grand paintings in rich colors with dream-like qualities.

Do something: Probably the best painter in this group to just stare at and ask, "How did he do that?"

Composition Mechanique

JOAN MIRÓ

Content: Think of Jackson Pollock doing an abstract rendering of the famous TV cartoon, the Jetsons and you can begin to get an idea of the fantasy world that Miró comes from. The amazing thing is that no matter how alien the colorful and shapely Miró blobs may seem at first, they somehow become endearing and familiar images from our world. If you are ever in New York City, visit MOMA, The Museum of Modern Art and see the strange and wonderful figures in the oil painting, "Person Throwing a Stone at a Bird."

Importance: Miró was a leading surrealist (the art movement that gave us the superstars like Dali. Remember the melting watch painting?) He is also one of the best selling popular painters in the world through his playful and colorful prints. Miró, along with Picasso, also provided the great city of Chicago with its most notable monumental sculptures. The

Adonides

Spanish born artist spent most of his time working in Paris and is truly a "world-wide" artist.

Style, format, appearance: Decorative, whimsical, colorful and always surprising. Perhaps Miró's own word's say it best, "For me, a picture should be like sparks. It must dazzle, like the beauty of a woman or a poem. It must have radiance. It must be like those stones which Pyrenean Shepherds used to light their pipes." Look out George Jetson!

Do something: Stare and make up stories about life on other planets and at home.

All Reflections Made in Times of Misery, the Mirror is Broke

CLAES OLDENBURG

Content: Everyday objects blown out of proportion. Giant hamburgers, clothespins and a thirty-foot high ice cream cone made from vinyl stuffed with Kapok (essentially giant beanbag chairs). Fun, engaging.

Importance: Responsible for some of the most remarkable and varied expressions of the American pop art movement.

Style, format, and appearance: Tongue in cheek stylized giant ordinary things. Extremely accessible and touchable sculptures. Vinyl, vivid colors, most very soft and pliable.

Do something: You'll want to touch most of his work and some you can. Most of his work is larger than life: human figures, heads with speech bubbles, animals, weapons, cars. See if you can guess what some of the more abstract ones are.

Spoonbridge and Cherry

Clothespin

JACKSON POLLOCK

Content: Abstracts. Non-representational.

Importance: Groundbreaker. One of the best-known 20th century artists.

Style, format, appearance: Abstracts. Large and easily viewed paintings that were dripped, splattered and stroked on canvas. Some used strong colors, others were monochromatic. Very textural and touchable. Some have his personal belongings stuck in the paint.

Do something: Okay, you won't be able to touch them but you'll feel almost like you can. Standing close you can almost feel the thickness of the paint and sometimes the things embedded in it. Great optical illusions. Stare at them and ask, "What in the world was he thinking?"

Number 6

Number 22

DAVID SMITH

Content: Metal sculptures. Abstract shapes. Non-objectionable.

Importance: One of the premier sculptors of the 20th century. Was a pioneer in the field of metal sculpture and monumental geometric construction.

Style, format, appearance: Great shiny robots. Fun, fun, fun. Large and accessible. Touch it, go ahead. Steel, iron, solder. As three dimensional as you can get.

Do something: Part of his sculpture's charm is in what they do. They become things like the toy transformers that kids love, both tangibly and in the viewer's imagination. It is great to walk around them and see how the different perspectives, changing light, and shadow patterns actually transform the image. Watch as you walk around one and see it change from a house into a rabbit.

Cube Totem Seven and Six

Gray Sundae by Claes Oldenburg

Chapter Three

About These Artists

It is interesting to note, as you become more familiar with these nine artists, that most of them took a very playful approach to their work. Their subject matter was very childlike and even in the few cases of the artists who were a little more serious, Kandinsky for example; they sought to express only inner and essential feelings and to ignore the superficial.

I have always felt that the greatest enjoyment in viewing any painting or sculpture is in the "feeling" I have when viewing it, in other words, the emotional aspects. Many times, when I am "moved" by a great work of art, I can't explain why; it's something intrinsic within the piece. Generally, those values of a piece of art that move me are the direct result of the emotion and passion that went into the creation of it. Somehow, I can feel the intensity, love or anger that went into the making of a particularly good work of art.

You've no doubt heard the statement, "I don't know much about art. I just know what I like," or words to that affect. And it is true that art can be appreciated without necessarily being "understood." In fact, I chose these nine artists for that very reason. However, to be "fully" appreciated, I have found that some investigation into the artist himself; a level of understanding about that person's life, passions, successes, trials or tribulations, increased my appreciation and regard for his work. Likewise, I most often find interesting parallels between the artist's life and my own.

It is my hope that this book will not only set you and your child on a new path of discovery and enjoyment, but that you will use this launch pad to further investigate these artists and their works and then others. As you become increasingly curious about them and their work and as you view additional works of theirs, you will find that you will begin to develop an "eye" as well as an appreciation for what they have created.

It is important, as you begin to visit various art museums, that you immerse yourself as much as possible in each piece. It's also important for you and your child to ask questions. Look at the various pieces as though they were living things. Why is something this way and something else that way? Why did the artist do this or that? Did the artist even mean to do something? Look at the works from different angles, up close, far away and soon you and your child will find that not only are you enjoying yourselves, you are learning something. You might even become a "connoisseur," but even if you don't, you and your child will have a great time.

ALEXANDER CALDER

American (1898–1976)

Calder pioneered the art of the mobile thereby becoming one of the founders of kinetic art. Talk about an artistic family, his grandfather and father were sculptors and his mother was a painter. Nevertheless, it took him more than twenty years to become interested in art, first studying mechanical engineering. He was born in Philadelphia, but in 1906, his family moved to Pasadena, California. At a young age, he became infatuated with the circus. He would create animals, figures and circus apparatus of wire and string and give performances in his room. He was also fascinated with the planets and stars, which became important to the imagery of his mobiles. It is said that his vivid recollections of trains, the San Francisco cable cars, and various toys played an important role in his later works as well.

He was perhaps the least "introspective" of this group of nine artists. He had a playful openness, at once naïve and self-confident. He was filled with a lively sense of wonder about the world.

His first sculpture was a sundial done in the form of a cockerel (a young rooster) in 1925. He also animated toys; his first exhibition of such was in New York in 1928. He and Joan (pronounced: Juan) Miró were great lifelong friends and each influenced the other's art to some degree.

In 1934 he began to work in the style for which he is best known, creating mobiles (the phrase was coined by his friend and fellow artist, Duchamp) and stabiles, which did not turn (the phrase was coined by his friend and artist, Jean Arp). He created these from shaped pieces of painted tin that were suspended by thin wires. This allowed the faintest air currents to randomly move the pieces, which then responded to the changing light conditions. He called them three-dimensional drawings. His sculptures created a constantly changing relationship of the solid objects used in the art and the spaces around them.

One of his most famous pieces entitled: ***Red, Black and Blue*** hangs in the Dallas Airport. Sadly, a monumental red painted steel sculpture, looking a bit like a bent propeller or the wings of a giant bird, was lost in 2001. It was on permanent display in the World Trade Center. It was said to have been worth $25 million.

Calder loved to "perform" a circus, which was a contraption/sculpture complete with animals and performers. He would open the performances by playing a scratchy recording on a gramophone. He would play the ringmaster (at the age of thirty-two). After making his announcements he would march each of the animals and performers into the arena with his huge hands, like a boy playing with toy soldiers. Most of his performance was done on his hands and knees and he would supply the sound effects including the voices of the animals and performers.

RED GROOMS

American (1937–   )

Grooms' art reflects his enjoyment of people and situations. His art included paper sculptures, "happenings," lithographs and even filmmaking. Well-known for his cartoon style, he is best known for his innovative 3-D paper portraits of notable people of the modern age, all infused with dry wit and a somewhat skewed sense of humor, part burlesque, part opera and that which is not easily categorized.

He once portrayed author and feminist, Gertrude Stein, sitting in a chintz-covered, over-stuffed chair as a paper construction made from two cutout, fold up lithographs he had created.

He studied art at the Chicago Art Institute and in 1959, he staged a "happening" in New York entitled, ***The House That Burns.*** A "happening" would have to be described more as an event. His was a mixture of Disneyland, vaudeville, and a Punch and Judy puppet show, part melodrama, and part protest. He was a good friend of Claes Oldenburg's who also helped Grooms stage some of his "happenings" as well as create many of his own.

A good example of Groom's humor was a walk-in exhibit on display at the McNay Art Museum in Fort Worth, Texas entitled, ***Ruckus Rodeo.*** A virtual cowgirl and cowboy's garden of delights unfolded as viewers passed through the exhibit. Greetings were made by a 10-foot tall rodeo queen on horseback waving the Texas flag as visitors were treated to a complete walk through rodeo alive with bleachers full of fans and anxious bulls waiting their turn behind the release gates. Critics said, "Highly rated for kids from five to ninety-five," it was originally completed for the Fort Worth Art Museum (now the Modern Art Museum of Fort Worth).

WASSILY KANDINSKY

Russian (1866–1944)

Kandinsky was a writer and a musician as well as a painter and is considered one of the most important pioneers of "abstract art." The next time you take your child to the museum to look at a Kadinsky, think about this: he gave up a career as a college professor, in part, because of the powerful impression that an exhibition in Moscow, of French Impressionists made upon him. In fact, one painting, a Monet entitled ***Haystack***, made an impression so lasting, in 1896 he left home to study painting in Munich, Germany.

Kandinsky wrote an essay about his art in 1913 entitled "Reminiscences." This portion deals with his first confrontation with impressionism:

> *I underwent two experiences which stamped my mind for life and which shook me to my marrow. They were the French Impressionist's exhibition in Moscow—particularly,* **Haystack,** *by Claude Monet—and a production of Wagner in the Lohengrin Theater.*
>
> *Previously I had only known realistic art, in fact, exclusively the Russians, having often stood for long periods before Repin's portrait of Franz Liszt. And now suddenly, for the first time, I saw a 'painting.' That it was a haystack, the catalogue had already informed me. I could not recognize it. This was painful to me.*

Kandinsky went on to describe how he was transfixed by this "new" art that was far from the realism he had always known. From that single experience, he returned home and vowed he would become an artist.

Kandinsky said his understanding of the power of non-representational art was derived from a night when he went into his studio in Munich and failed to recognize one of his own paintings that was lying the "wrong" way up, seeing in it a picture of "extraordinary beauty glowing with an inner radiance."

He wrote in more detail about this occurrence in 1913:

> *Much later, after my arrival in Munich, I was enchanted on one occasion by an unexpected spectacle that confronted me in my studio. It was the hour when dusk draws in. I returned home with my painting box having finished a study, still dreamy and absorbed in the work I had completed, and suddenly saw an indescribably beautiful picture, pervaded by an inner glow. At first, I stopped short and then quickly approached this mysterious picture, on which I could discern only forms and colors and whose content was incomprehensible. At once, I discovered the key to the puzzle: it was a picture that I had painted, standing on its side against the wall.*
>
> *The next day, I tried to re-create my impression of the picture from the previous evening. I only half succeeded, however: even on its side, I constantly recognized objects that were now missing in the fine bloom of dusk. Now I could see clearly that objects harmed my pictures.*

Kandinsky is often cited as the first person to paint an abstract picture. In 1914 he returned to Russia where he became a distinguished academic. In 1921 he once again left Russia to teach at the famous Bauhaus in Germany where he remained until it closed in 1933. Eventually he settled permanently in Paris becoming a citizen in 1939.

Kadinsky held that the "pure" artist seeks to express only inner and essential feelings and ignores the superficial and fortuitous—not unlike a child's view of art. He was also a musician.

He thought of colors as music. Simple pictures were like little melodies to him. Complex paintings were like symphonies. He even called many of his paintings "improvisations," meaning a song made up on the spot. Young artists can enjoy the music of colors by letting imaginations fly while painting to the music.

FERNAND LÉGER

French (1881–1955)

Fernand was a painter and a designer. He was generally considered a master cubist though his curvilinear and tubular forms won him the tongue in cheek title of "tubist." His paintings were monumental in style and were always concerned with the contrast between cylindrical and rectilinear forms, in particular, machines.

Much of his inspiration was the result of his participation in World War I during which time he was gassed, serving as a stretcher-bearer. His contact with men of different social classes and walks of life had a profound effect on him and was the reason he made it his ambition to make his life's work accessible to the average man and woman (and child). Between the two World Wars, he expanded his easel painting to include murals and designs for the theatre and cinema and was a teacher at his own school, the Academie de L'Art Contemporain.

He traveled widely, visiting the U.S. in the 1930s. During the Second World War, he lived in the U.S., teaching at Yale University and Mills College in California. He returned to France in 1945 where his paintings began to reflect his political interest in the working classes. Much of his art was concerned with everyday objects and the intrinsic beauty of modern machinery. However, his war experiences changed his life and his art. It was during this time that he abandoned cubism. After his discharge, he had this to say:

> *Three years spent without touching a brush, but in contact with the rawest, most violent reality. As soon as I was demobilized, I benefited from those harsh years: I reached a decision and began to paint using pure tones, clearly defined colors and huge masses, making no concessions. I progressed beyond tidy, tasteful arrangements, muted grayish tones and dead surfaces in the background. I stopped floundering; I saw things clearly. I am not afraid to say candidly that the war brought about my fulfillment.*

It is interesting to note the life experiences that influenced these artists, in particular Léger, and how that translates to his art. In this case, what could have been a negative (war) becomes a positive. The conspicuous embodiment of modern civilization becomes his central concern. His unflagging optimism and radical faith in the future are manifested in the large figurative paintings and the perfection of the illustration of gigantic machines.

ROY LICHTENSTEIN

American (1923–1997)

Lichtenstein was born in New York and studied at the Art Students' League and at Ohio State University, Columbus. Between 1949 and 1951, he taught at Ohio State University and in 1951, he had his first one-man exhibition at the Carlebach Gallery in New York.

Until 1957, he worked as a commercial artist and graphic designer and created displays for department store windows. He was a keen observer of "life's little ironies." The paintings he did during this time were parodies of the art of the twenties in America, e.g., Remington's cowboy and Indian bronzes and for a time, he went through a non-representational period of abstract and expressionist styles.

In 1960, he became acquainted with Claes Oldenburg and began to use the elements of his graphic arts background, using comics and advertising in his drawings and paintings.

In 1963, he was commissioned by the architect, Philip Johnson, to produce large format paintings for the New York State Pavilion at the World's Fair in New York and had his first one-man exhibition in Paris.

Lichtenstein expressed his feelings with complete detachment. His fierce anti-pictorial style highlights "technique" at the expense of content. He derived and parodied the images of pulp magazines and comics and was particularly interested in the lack of sensitivity in mass produced images and merchandising art. This prompted him to mimic such aspects of the public landscape in his work. Corny, popular romance characters, travel poster vulgarizations and comic book heroes dominate his art.

This is what Lichtenstein had to say about his art:

> *I think it (my art) merely portrays it (society). One would hardly look at my work and think that it wasn't satirical, I think, or that it made no comment. But I don't really think that I'm interested in making a social comment. I'm using these aspects of our environment,*

> *which I talked about as subject matter, but I'm interested in doing a painting. No doubt, this has an influence on my work somehow, but I'm not sure what social message my art carries, if any. And I don't really want it to carry one. I'm not interested in the subject matter to try to teach society anything, or to try to better our world in any way.*

Lichtenstein is a realist. He captures the collective conscious of his day, or rather the way in which it is informed by the essence and language of the mass media, and yet he does not pass judgment.

JOAN MIRÓ

Spanish (1893–1983)

Miró was multi-talented, a painter, sculptor, graphic artist and designer. He was influenced by Picasso and cubism but was always associated with surrealism. He believed in releasing the creative forces of his subconscious mind from the control of logic and reason, much as a child does. One of the first works where he displayed this vision was entitled ***Harlequin's Carnival***, which featured a bizarre assembly of insect-like creatures dancing and making music, a scene he said, was inspired by the hallucinations brought on by hunger. Much of Miró's work has the delightful quality of playfulness seen in the ***Harlequin's Carnival.***

He fled Spain for Paris in 1936 because of the Spanish Civil War, but returned in 1940 in order to escape Nazi occupation of France. He worked with a great deal of energy for the rest of his life, in a variety of fields. In 1944, he began making ceramics and slightly later, he took up sculpture, eventually working with large-scale pieces for casting in bronze.

In 1947, he visited the U.S. for the first time and completed a large mural for the Terrace Hilton Hotel in Cincinnati. In another effort to make his work widely accessible, he took up printmaking (etchings and lithographs) that would be more affordable to the average citizen. Later he experimented with stained glass designs, ceramics, sculpture, printmaking (etchings and lithographs) well into his eighties.

In spite of his worldwide fame, he was a modest, retiring character, completely devoted to his work.

CLAES OLDENBURG

Swedish (1929–)

Oldenburg became an American citizen in 1953 and was educated at Yale University and the Art Institute of Chicago, at times earning a living as a part time reporter on a police beat and as an illustrator. In 1956 he settled in New York where he came in contact with a group of artists who were in revolt against abstract expressionism and from that time on, he became involved with arranging "happenings," which could best be described as situations, environments or activities. He is known best for using everyday common objects as the focus of his work.

His inspiration was largely drawn from New York's street life—shop windows, graffiti, advertisements, etc., and in 1961, he opened The Store, at which he sold painted plaster or plastic replicas of foods and other domestic objects. This led to the work, with which he is most closely associated—giant-size soft sculptures of everyday familiar forms—disproportionate surrogates with life of their own—enlarged to grotesque proportions and bearing unnatural shape and consistency, they are clear allusions to the perishable and temporary nature of consumer objects.

His soft sculptures were created by stitching vinyl and other fabrics together and then stuffing them with kapok (bean bag chair filler). Some of his subject matter included a giant twenty- foot tall ice cream cone, a work entitled ***Dual Hamburgers, Lipsticks in Picadilly Circus.*** One of his largest projects was the monumental seventy-foot high ***Match Cover*** that was erected in Barcelona, Spain in 1992.

JACKSON POLLOCK

American (1912–1956)

What child would not relate to Jackson Pollock, particularly the "drip and splash" techniques that he used in later years? Instead of using the traditional easel, he laid his canvas on the floor, poured, and dripped his paint right out of the can using commercial enamels and metallic paint, which he felt better suited his purposes (and were probably quite a bit cheaper than artist's oils, at least in the large quantities that he used).

Rather than using a brush, Pollock manipulated the paint with sticks, trowels or knives, sometimes arriving at textured effects by adding sand, broken glass or other foreign matter to the paints. In some cases he poured, dripped or dropped the paint onto a canvas on the floor and then tilted the canvas up to allow the paint to run and form random shapes. He had a sort of "hand to hand" encounter with the surfaces to be painted and felt that his work could only be obtained by starting from a sort of "state of grace." The term, automatism partially applies to his thinking. That is when one aims to express his or her true creative unconscious with the absence of any control, reason or aesthetic.

His style was caught up in the "all over" approach in which he tried to avoid any points of emphasis on particular areas or related parts. Samuel Butler once said, "Life is like learning how to play the violin and having to give concerts at the same time." That is how Pollock painted, as if living and painting were the same. He either got it right or he blew it, losing himself in the self-indulgence of it.

Pollock's unhappy personal life and his premature death in 1956 at the height of his popularity, contributed to his status as one of the legends of modern art; he was the first American painter to become a "star." Of course, he wasn't always a star. Early in his career during his first exhibition at "Art of this Century" in New York, he was showing a collage. His name was misspelled "Pollach" on the exhibition announcement and his showing went unnoticed by the press, save for one critic who wrote a very brief review calling the work, "Nice." The collage didn't sell, the show closed quickly and Pollock went home and threw the painting away. It was the last time however, that he would go unnoticed.

Early in his career, Pollock had this to say about his art:

> *My painting does not come from the easel. I hardly ever stretch my canvas before painting. I prefer to tack the unstretched canvas to the hard wall or the floor because I need the resistance of the hard surface. On the floor, I'm more at ease. I feel nearer, more a part of the painting, since this way, I can walk around it, work from the four sides and literally be "in" the painting.*

> *This is akin to the method of the Indian sand painters of the West. I continue to get further away from the usual painter's tools such as easel, palette, brushes, etc. I prefer sticks, trowels, knives and dripping fluid paint or a heavy impasto with sand, broken glass and other foreign matter added. When I am "in" my painting, I am not aware of what I am doing. It is only after a sort of 'get acquainted' period that I see what I have been about. I have no fears of making changes, destroying the image, etc., because the painting has a life of its own. I try to let it come through. It is only when I lose contact with the painting that the result is a mess. Otherwise there is pure harmony, an easy give and take, and the painting comes well.*

I don't know about you, but just reading what Pollock said about his technique makes me want to look at his work. I want to see the result of so much energy and pure passion.

DAVID SMITH

American (1906–1965)

Born in Decatur, Indiana, Smith first attended Ohio University, Athens and then moved to New York in 1926, determined to become an artist. He was perhaps the most original and influential American sculptor of his generation.

While in the middle of his studies at Ohio University in 1924, he dropped out and in the summer of 1925, he worked at the Studebaker motor plant at South Bend, Indiana, where he acquired the metalworking skills that he used throughout his life.

Some of Smith's work in the early 1930s was created using scraps of things he found and old agricultural machinery. For a time, he made a living as a welder on defense work but returned to sculpture in 1945 after World War II. In the 1940s and 1950s, his work was open and linear almost like three-dimensional metal calligraphy.

From the end of the 1950s up until his death in a car accident, he did the more massive works for which he is best known. Though monumental and intended to be seen in the open, these last works, known as "cubis," characteristically consisted of boxes and cylinders of polished metal, which had a dynamic quality—in many cases they resemble giant robots.

Applause by David Smith

Chapter Four

Introducing Your Children to Art

Why is it important to enjoy and understand art? You will be astounded at the impact that art can have on the lives of your children, and your own. As you progress through this book and begin to involve art in your life more you will begin to see how it can:

- Generate joy and fun!
- Provide solace/ Serve as an emotional release
- Help you to understand yourself more/Strengthen self-concept and confidence/Increase self-understanding
- Provide inspiration and stimulate creativity
- Help you connect to your world/Develop appreciation for the individuality of others/Lead to the integration of the individual

- Provide a means of communication and self-expression
- Heighten aesthetic awareness and sensitivity/Enhance the ability to visualize
- Provide problem-solving/decision-making opportunities
- Aid physical coordination

WOW! That's a lot of good stuff, but it's all true.

If art can truly provide these benefits to your child and you, and I contend that it does, how can you not at least explore the possibilities a little further? Let's discuss each of these benefits briefly:

GENERATES JOY AND FUN

We've all heard of IQ (Intelligence Quotient). It has been the predictor of your child's mental ability, or the potential to learn. According to Stevanne Auerbach, Ph.D., in her book ***Dr. Toy's Smart Play,*** " . . . your child's PQ or Play Quotient, is an equally vital factor, which affects how well your young one will attain the best of his physical, creative, and intellectual potentials."

Dr. Auerbach goes on to say, "Play is your child's work. Through play, children practice the basic skills needed in the classroom—and in life."

Dr. Auerbach continues at length about the importance of play as it relates to social, mental and neurological development. If you are interested in this subject, I highly recommend her book. In the interest of time however, and for our purposes here, let us just agree that play is important to a child's development. The question we are concerned with is: What is playful about enjoying art? There are the obvious things when applied to the nine artists in this book including: the ability to touch and feel the textures and shapes of much of their work, the stimulus that the visual reactions create (e.g. smiles, laughter, excitement), and the discovery of what led the artists to create their work.

I think we all want our children to play with others of different ages and abilities so that they may experience the interactions of patience, empathy, compassion and honesty. Likewise, our children should experience the interactions of different artistic visual stimuli and of course, the ensuing dialogue that takes place between parent and child while enjoying the art together.

PROVIDES SOLACE

Art can be a refuge from the pressures of modern life for you and your children. I think you would agree that there is precious little time in today's world for reflection and peace and quiet. Art can provide this inexpensively and easily. Artist, Henri Matisse, once observed, "I want to create an art that might be so comforting that tired businessmen would readily turn to it for solace." If you ever have the opportunity to look at his two works: ***Red Studio*** or ***Luxe, Calme et Volupte*** in New York's Museum of Modern Art, I think you'll agree that he succeeded.

For years, medicine and science have recognized the therapeutic effect of art. Enjoying art is a safety valve by which an individual can drain off tensions. Children that turn "emotions" into creative channels have a more acceptable outlet for those emotions. Painting is a form of playing things out. Seeing and enjoying another individual's painting is also a form of playing things out in the mind.

UNDERSTANDING YOURSELF MORE

Art can help your children understand themselves more. When you get to Chapter 7, Art and Your Life, you will see how parts of the artists' lives may well mirror your own life in terms of your goals, desires, successes and setbacks. How these artists dealt with their own trials, may well provide answers in your own life, or at least provide a place to begin.

Looking at, understanding, and creating art, are all instruments of self-discovery. As children gradually begin to understand and enjoy art, they begin to discover other's (artist's) points of view, different from their own. This also enables them to develop their own opinions. Their choices of subject matter, materials and colors will be revealing to you and to them.

PROVIDES INSPIRATION AND STIMULATES CREATIVITY

Enjoying art and understanding what inspired a particular artist to create a painting, a drawing, or a sculpture, can be extremely inspiring and most certainly will lead your child to greater creativity on his or her own.

We will discuss the power of creative thinking in another chapter in more detail. Your child can learn to be more creative ***observing, experiencing*** and ***doing***. To promote creativity, a parent should provide all these opportunities. With many of the artists we've chosen in this first volume, there is what I call an "I can do that factor" and you will see what I mean by that when we begin to discuss and view each of these artist's work at the end of this chapter.

HELPS YOU AND YOUR CHILD CONNECT TO YOUR WORLD

By viewing the work of others, your child learns to appreciate different ideas and he or she begins to understand that there is more than one way to do just about everything. This fosters a greater empathy for others and helps your child to connect to the world. Now, more than ever before, it is important for people to understand each other more keenly. It is difficult to hate someone you understand. An understanding of others fosters more tolerance and empathy.

Likewise, discussions between you and your child will help you connect with each other and provide a rich outlet for ongoing dialogue.

As your child grows older, he will be able to share his enjoyment and understanding of art with others, in social, business and personal settings.

In fact, have you ever noticed how the "successful" people in the world all seem to share an interest in the arts? In past eras, one of the necessary and required elements of a good education was the study and appreciation of art. Oddly enough, in past centuries, only nobility had access to it. The paradox is that originally, everyone wanted access, but only the rich had it. Now, everyone has access, but in great part, only the wealthy avail themselves. It's time to change all that.

The process of integration leads to a balanced individual because we all understand our world through three functions: ***movement, thoughts*** and ***emotions.*** Art can be a prominent key to unlocking all of these. The child and adult that balances all three becomes a better-integrated individual.

PROVIDES A MEANS OF COMMUNICATION AND EXPRESSION

Enjoying and learning about art first provides the basis for a parent/child dialogue, we discussed this in chapter one. However, the enjoyment of art can provide the stimulus for communication between your child and the rest of the world as well.

As she grows older and becomes involved in increasingly more complex social situations (personal, business, social), the bank of information, learning and understanding that was gained at an early age and hopefully continues through life, provides your child with an endless source of conversational topics. You may remember an advertisement from the early 1960s that ran for quite some time. I think the headline read, "They all laughed . . . until I sat down to play the piano."

HEIGHTENS AESTHETIC AWARENESS AND SENSITIVITY/ ENHANCES THE ABILITY TO VISUALIZE

Experiencing art sharpens all the senses. It makes us more literate visually. This awareness then spills over into an awareness of our total environment, from the furniture in our homes, to clothing, architecture, and indeed, the entire world. The functional level that an individual achieves is a direct reflection of the stimulation and opportunities afforded to that person. Stimulation leads to awareness, which in turn causes your children to become more perceptive interpreters of their world.

Visualization, or the ability to see a picture in the mind's eye, is not only a vital aspect of the creative process, it is a technique used by all successful individuals in their attempts to reach goals. Professional athletes are prime examples of people who have taken visualization to an art form. As an example,

Mark McGwire, the star of the St. Louis Cardinals who achieved the astounding record of hitting seventy home runs in a single season in 1999, says that every time he goes to bat he first visualizes an entire scene beginning with the release of the ball from the pitcher's hand, to it's journey in his direction, to his bat striking the ball all the way to following the flight of the ball into the upper decks of left field. He envisions this scene before he even steps up to the plate and apparently, judging by his success, it works. Successful businessmen and women, musicians and artists do the same type of thing.

Why is this so important? Because the ability to see an action or a picture in your mind's eye, is vital to becoming a clear thinker. Setting and achieving goals and being able to see in advance the results of your actions, and then knowing that you ***can*** achieve whatever you can conceive, is fundamental to accomplishment. It's also a practice that can weed out mistakes and disappointments before they occur.

PROVIDES PROBLEM-SOLVING/ DECISION-MAKING OPPORTUNITIES

Building on the last statement, the ability to visualize a situation or a problem before engaging in an activity helps to eliminate mistakes. Visualization isn't just goal setting, it is an evaluation process. All of this begins with "seeing" things as they are and as they can be. Viewing and enjoying art is both. By looking at art and questioning what motivated an artist to do what he did and then visualizing how it might look in different colors, using different textures, is just one example of the physical process of becoming aware, becoming sensitive and learning to visualize what could be.

AIDS PHYSICAL COORDINATION/ THE IMPORTANCE OF VISUAL PURSUITS

The term "visual pursuits" refers to the coordination of the eyes as they move up and down, back and forth in reading or following objects. For one eye to move smoothly the cooperation and coordination of six muscles are needed; twelve muscles for both eyes. For most of us, these movements are involuntary and our eyes work quite well. However, for some children, especially those who have reading problems, this may be a serious challenge. Losing one's place frequently while reading can be the result of poor eye muscle coordination. Omitting words and/or substituting words can also be a result of this condition.

In order for the eyes of young children to learn to converge and to work together, it is necessary to look at fixed objects with frequency, intensity and duration. Viewing art from a fixed distance is a great exercise, particularly for very young children, to strengthen these muscle groups and to develop good depth perception. All of which leads to one of the reasons we become coordinated physically, or we grow up to be less than coordinated, because the proper convergence of the eyes and good depth perception contribute greatly to our overall balance.

THE POWER OF MEMORIES

Doing art

An old proverb states: "I *hear* and I forget. I *see* and I remember. I *do* and I understand."

It is important to *do* as well as to observe and it can be full of fun as well. I feel we should enable our children to express what they see, not only verbally, but also by doing. *Doing* further empowers children. It gives voice to what appeals to them. It is a way of telling their stories by rendering what they perceive through physical gesture. As I said earlier, observation and imitation are two of our most powerful learning techniques. What better way to "do" than to create some art using some of our Nine Famous Artists as examples, using the same media and tools they used?

The reason I've done this is not only to provide a fun activity that you and your child can do together, and for your child to learn something new, or even to further relate to the works of these artists; I have done it for those reasons and more, for the "power of memories."

Memories can be inspiring. As I already mentioned, Kandinsky's memory of a single painting caused him to give up a promising career and focus on a new one. Many famous actors vividly recall creating fantasy dramas for their parents and neighbors when they were children. Some teachers relate that they decided to go into their profession because they remember the scenes they played at home, the scenes of playing school.

It is therefore quite possible that after you have viewed the works of some or all of these artists, and you've had the opportunity to play with your child in creating pieces of art in similar fashions, you will be creating memories to last a lifetime, perhaps even to inspire something very special in your child.

In their book, ***Discovering Great Artists,*** MaryAnn F. Kohl and Kim Solga have created a wonderful series of hands-on art projects based on the great masters that you and your child can create right in your own kitchen. You can find their book in most major booksellers. We've included three of the projects from that book. Have fun!

ALEXANDER CALDER was an American sculptor. (See pages 23, 24, 71 and 72 for examples of his work.) As a child, he enjoyed making things from old dishes and pieces of wire. He also loved to make contraptions from his collections of scraps and junk. Mobiles can hang from the ceiling or stand freely.

Here is an afternoon project that your child will love. In this project, you and your child can make a mobile using a simple block of Styrofoam and scraps from around the house or garage.

Creating a Standing Mobile

Materials:

- Craft wire (telephone cable also works)
- Styrofoam packing block
- Bits of colored paper, foil, stickers, cardboard
- Glue or tape
- Scissors

Process:

- Cut craft wire to any length desired.
- Stick the wire into the top of the block of Styrofoam. The wire can be bent into wiggly shapes or left straight.

- Add more wire in the block.
- Tape or glue bits of paper to the wires like flags or flowers. Stickers work well too.

WASSILY KANDINSKY, in addition to being a painter, was also a musician. (See pages 26, 27 and 73 for examples of his work.) He thought of colors as music. Simple pictures were like little melodies to him. Complex paintings were like symphonies. He even called many of his paintings "improvisations," meaning a song made up on the spot. Young artists can enjoy the music of colors by letting their imaginations fly while painting to the music.

Here is something fun that you and your children can experiment with on a Sunday afternoon. I call it "Painting by Music," it was inspired by Kandinsky. You'll need some materials and a table. The dining room or kitchen table will work just fine.

Painting Music

Materials:

- Watercolors, tempera or acrylic paints
- Paintbrushes
- Paper, canvas or illustration board
- A source of music, tapes, CDs or records. And you'll need some music, e.g., Bach, Wagner, Ravel, Copeland, Sant-Sens, Grofe (or for that matter anything you care to choose).

Process:

- Listen to the music for five or ten minutes without doing anything. Try closing your eyes. As you're listening, try to imagine what colors, lines or shapes could be used to illustrate the emotions that the music creates.

- Now listen to the music again while painting a picture of the sounds. Use lines, colors and shapes to draw any particular object or just create abstract designs. In other words, improvise. Don't plan what you are sketching.
- Now change the music and try it all over again.
- Place the mobile by a window and watch in move with the air currents. The gentle push of a finger can set the mobile in motion as well.

ROY LICHTENSTEIN was a fine artist, a graphic designer and an art teacher. (See pages 28, 29 and 74 for examples of his work.) He used his advertising background to create his art called pop op. Much of his art is based on advertising and comic book images. Many of his pieces are very large. His art is created using a connection of dots and color and they often include a white "talk-balloon," so that his characters can talk to the viewer. He liked to use the words, "Wham! Boom! Zap! Blam!"

Comic Dots

Materials

- Comic books or newspaper cartoons from the Sunday morning paper
- Magnifying glass
- Large sheet of butcher paper, about 4′ x 8′ taped to the wall
- Pencil
- Tempera paints in red, yellow, black or other (Put them in flat baking trays)

- Sponges, about 1/2" across
- Marking pen or paintbrush

Process

- Look at a cartoon or comic with a magnifying glass. Note the tiny dots. See how the dots are different colors. Take away the magnifying glass and look at the comic again. See how the colors and dots blend to create images?
- Sketch a simple comic idea on the butcher paper; one frame or box is enough. Make it simple. Draw and outline the basic features of the character and other objects in the cartoon. Now draw a talk-balloon above the character's head and write in whatever you wish.
- Now apply dots of paint about 1" apart filling in the character's shape. You can refer back to one of Roy Lichtenstein's paintings in this book to help you. Just be sure to use dots, no lines.
- As the painting dries, stand back and look at it. The further back you get, the more the dots will appear to blend. Kablam! Looks good.

JACKSON POLLOCK, at times, involved his entire body in his "action" paintings, dripping, splattering, throwing paint onto the canvas. (See pages 36, 37 and 77 for examples of his work.) No, we don't suggest you use your entire body and splatter paint all over your kitchen. Instead, let's do a mini splatter project. As I described earlier, Jackson used brushes, sticks and his fingers to literally throw paint at the canvas. He even incorporated some of his own personal things by sticking them into the wet paint and even added his handprints. He was the original finger painter.

He once said that when he was painting, he was "in" the paintings and did not fear destroying the work because the work had a life of its own. Let's do an action splatter.

Action Spatter

Materials

- Newspaper covered work area (about the size of your kitchen table)
- A cardboard box with one side cut away
- Old clothes or overalls
- A variety of large brushes
- Large containers of tempera paint
- Large craft paper or newsprint

Process

- Cover the work area with newspapers. Tape the paper so the sheets stay in place. Put the box on the newspaper, with the opening facing the artist. Note: It might be a good idea to do this in the garage or on the grass. At any rate, tempera is a water-based paint and will clean up quite easily with soap and water.
- Place a sheet of craft paper inside the box. Tape if necessary.
- Cover the artist with old clothing or coverall to allow for "freedom" from concern about ruing good clothing (very important).
- Put on some music with a strong beat e.g. Latin, jazz or rock and roll (optional).

- Begin by dipping a large brush into a container of paint.
- Hold the brush inside the box and splatter the paint onto the paper by shaking the brush from up to down in one large motion.
- Add more colors and more spattering.
- Load up paintbrush and hold above the paper allowing paint to slowly drip, keep your hand moving.
- Allow extra drying time due to thickness of paint. Take paper out of box and allow to flatten.

DAVID SMITH was a metal sculptor who once said: "If it's out in the barn, weld it together!" (See pages 38 and 78 for examples of his work.) Among his many monumental geometric pieces he is well known for a series called, ***Primary Structure*** in his "cubi" series; essentially three large cubes of steel welded together to form a tack sitting on top of single cylinders of steel.

You and your child can have fun on a smaller scale by using wooden blocks and glue. The possibility for shapes and sizes are endless.

Cubi Structure

Materials

- Wood scraps and wooden blocks (blocks can be purchased at school supply stores)
- White glue (electric craft glue gun, only with adult supervision)
- Cardboard square or flat piece of wood for base
- Paints and brushes (optional)
- Masking tape

Process

- Collect wood scraps from wood shop or purchase.
- Glue a cylinder or rectangle to the base to form a standing post as the central support of the structure. Allow to dry briefly
- Glue more blocks or cylinders to the post, standing them on edge, balancing or building and gluing in any style suitable to the artist.
- If necessary, add masking tape to temporarily hold the pieces in place until it dries completely. Remove any masking tape
- If desired, paint the cubi sculpture with tempera or watercolor paints.

I'm sure if you review the art of the other Famous Artists in this book, using the aforementioned examples as guidelines, you and your children should be able to come up with some great projects, based on their art as well, on your own.

Etching with Star, Boat and Waves by Alexander Calder

Alexander Calder

Wassily Kandinsky

Cubist Still Life in the Manner of Cezanne by Roy Lichtenstein

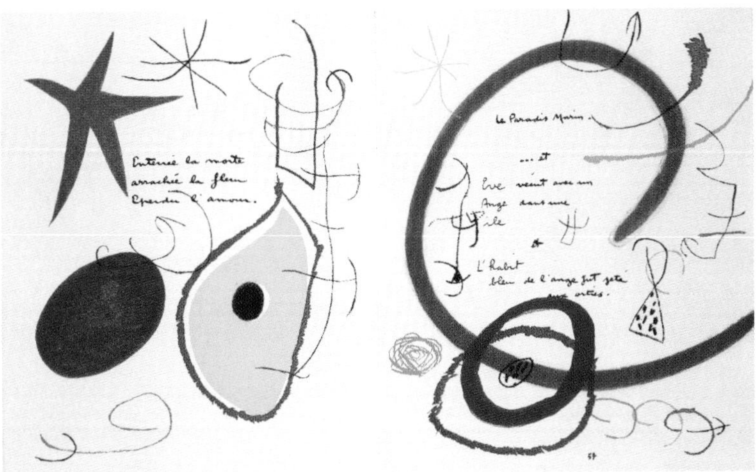
Enterrée la morte
arrachée la fleur
éperdu l'amour.
le Paradis Marin.
... et
Eve venait avec un
Ange dans une
île
&
L'habit
bleu de l'ange fut jeté
aux orties.

Joan Miró

Claes Oldenburg

Jackson Pollock

VB XXIII by David Smith

Cubist Still Life in the Manner of Cezanne
by Roy Lichtenstein

Chapter Five

How to Experience the Museum Like a Pro on Your First Visit

We've talked at length about the many benefits of enjoying art and we've even created some. Now it's time to go see some. The weekend is coming. It's time to plan your first visit to your local museum or art gallery. What should you do? Unless you live in a rural area, your city will most likely have a museum or art gallery, perhaps more than one. What should you do before you pack up the kids and jump in the car? Here is a checklist to help you get started.

PREPARING FOR THE DAY

In the back of this book is a listing of some of the major galleries and museums in the United States. You may find their phone numbers, addresses and web sites quite helpful.

Keep in mind that museums often keep odd hours. Some are open all weekend and closed on Mondays and Tuesdays. Others only open after noontime. Also, museums often have "free days," so it is best to call ahead to get as much information as possible before leaving. The good part is that museums are usually open on weekends when people have the time to visit.

Most importantly, act enthusiastic about your pending trip. Your excitement is contagious.

ASK QUESTIONS

When you call the museum use the opportunity to ask some important questions. Since this first volume contains nine specific artists, ask if any of them are included in the exhibits. If so, ask if the specific pieces are appropriate for children. If they are not exhibiting any of these artists, or the work would not be appropriate, ask them to suggest another venue. Most of the time, the museum staff is delighted to help you enjoy art and they will be quite helpful. In fact, they are among the nicest and most helpful people in the world.

If the museum is not exhibiting any of these artists, but you want to go anyway (which I wholeheartedly encourage), ask the staff if they have any children's art. Be sure to be specific. You're not looking for art that was *created* by children; you're looking for art that would *appeal* to a child perhaps six to twelve.

WHAT ELSE DO THEY OFFER?

As long as you're asking questions, inquire about their facilities. Most museums have restaurants inside or at least snack bars. Make a day of it, plan your visit near the lunch hour, and enjoy a meal there as well.

Nearly every museum in the country also has a gift shop. Make sure to stop by after you've toured the exhibits. The gift shops are a great source for further reading on these artists and art in general. They also generally carry reproductions of the art in the form of posters, postcards or prints. If your child has shown a particular interest in an artist, and you can afford it (postcards and small posters are usually reasonably priced) then by all means, buy your child a reproduction. This can make for additional conversation later. It helps to keep the fun and the learning going. Let your child be the first kid on the block to have a Jackson Pollock poster hanging in his room.

I remember when growing up, I loved my grandmother and I was always fascinated with the Renoir reproduction she had hanging on the wall in her living room. Unfortunately, or fortunately, depending upon how you look at it, when I asked for more information about this artist on several occasions, my grandmother did not offer much information so I took it upon myself to find out more about this French Impressionist. This single piece of art stimulated me enough to spend hours in research and subsequently was one of the early inspirations that led to a life of discovery about art.

The word "museum" comes from the Greek word "mouseion," which translates to "a temple to the Muses." In Greek mythology, Zeus had nine beautiful daughters who never grew old. They were called the Muses and inspired creativity. Even today, artists and writers ask the Muses to inspire them.

I hope you will look forward to your visit for inspiration as well.

WHAT SHOULD YOU BRING?

Make sure to pack this book. Use it as a reference during your visit. If one or more of the artists in here are on exhibit, you can refresh your memory and that of your child's. Use it as a resource. Look for some of the art that is reproduced in this book and note in here some of the parallels between the artist's life and your own.

It's a good idea to take some paper and a pen or pencil as well as a small tape recorder. You can note your child's likes and dislikes. Note the questions your child asks for future discussion.

WHAT SHOULD YOU DO?

It is a good idea to remind yourself that your first priority is to have fun. Don't try to overwhelm your children with the academics of the art. Just relax and watch them experience the work. See the joy in their eyes and share it with them. Believe me, you'll be thrilled with their reactions and questions. Ask them what they think about the art. It might be the first time they have been rewarded with an adult conversation.

Start your trip by being excited. Affect a fun attitude for what you are about to do together. Tell your children you're going to do something that is fun and exciting. Tell them you're going to a visual amusement park. In other words, avoid telling them that you are going to "learn" something. Be enthusiastic! If you get into it, your kids will too. Lead by your energetic example, it's contagious.

One of the first things you can do to orient yourself is to go to the information booth. They are quite helpful and they can guide you to what you're looking for. Ask them if there are any special exhibits and if there are any of these artists exhibiting. Ask if they provide audio tours. (You will be given a tape player along with headsets to wear as you are guided throughout the exhibits). This is a great way to have a first time experience. Ask the staff for a map of the museum so that you can get oriented right away.

After you've read this book and perhaps done some further research on your own, you should be quite familiar with each of these nine artists. On your first visit, your child may just stare at a piece with an inquisitive look, so be prepared through your reading and understanding to create your own stories about a particular piece of art or a part of the artist's life.

Research has shown that the average museum visitor spends just four seconds looking at an object. Children tend to have even shorter attention spans, preferring the sounds, smells and the looks on other people's faces, to the paintings. For this reason, the parent and child usually do not come away with a "shared looking" experience.

In order to get the most out of your museum visit, I suggest the first visit be two hours or less if you are taking a young child. It's easy to overload on images and become more worn out than excited. Also, you may want to limit the number of paintings and/or sculptures you view to ten or less. Looking at too many pictures encourages brain fade. Try to concentrate on fewer visuals and spend more time with each, asking your child questions and discussing them. In this manner, both of you will come away with at least one or two "shared looking" experiences that you will remember and will be able to continue to discuss.

You can enjoy a work of art for as long as it takes to smell an orange. Then, to keep your interest, you have to do something more.

— Sir Kenneth Clark,
British Art Historian

Most works in a museum are labeled. The label usually lists the artist's name first, and then his nationality and birth date followed by the title of the work, the medium that was used and how the museum acquired the work. This information alone is worth jotting down on your note pad. However, I have found that occasionally, it's fun not to look at the label, but instead to try to guess who the artist is and what the medium was.

HOW TO LOOK AT A PIECE OF ART

Of course there is really no right or wrong way to look at a piece of art but these tips could prove helpful, especially as a newcomer and particularly for children.

Let your eyes wander over the entire surface. Absorb what you are looking at. Remember, for these moments, **this incredible piece of art belongs to you.** It is important to spend time with it, because there is usually more than meets the eye after an initial engagement.

Now, after you've spent a few moments looking at the piece, turn away for a minute, wait a few seconds, turn back, and view it again. Most often, you will see something new, kind of like seeing a movie for the second time.

Next, look for shapes, lines and perspective. Shapes that are close together like triangles, circles and squares tend to add energy to the artwork. Shapes that are further apart look more serene.

Look for lines. These could be obvious lines or they could be where two shapes, tones or color butt up against one another. Diagonal lines tend to create more action than horizontal lines. Vertical lines often create a sense of strength and stability or balance.

Artists use perspective to make two-dimensional surfaces look as if they had depth (three-dimensional). An artist will use certain tricks to create these illusions. For example, objects that are smaller and less detailed will appear to be off in the distance. Background colors are usually lighter to give the same impression. Parallel lines, like two railroad tracks running into the horizon, will create the illusion of space.

Many of the works in this book contain no perspective at all because they are abstract in nature. However, you will undoubtedly be viewing works by a wide variety of artists on your museum visit, so you can discuss these things with your children as well. When people first began to paint well up until the Renaissance period, they did not understand perspective or how to create the illusion of three dimensions. If you see some of these paintings on your visit, you will readily see how oddly flat everything appears. It will look as if all of the people illustrated in the picture are all standing in the foreground. Lines do not converge, as railroad tracks appear to, and many of the colors and tones were all equal, as well.

If you do indeed get the opportunity on your museum visit to see a Calder mobile or a David Smith sculpture or a Claes

Oldenburg soft sculpture, try to look at it with these thoughts in mind:

Surface, scale and space—Is the surface the same everywhere? Is the scale life-size? How much space do you need to look at it?

Conditions—Has the environment changed the piece? Has time?

Light—Is the sculpture the same color all over? Are there reflections? If there are reflections, do they change as you walk around the piece?

Place—Was this piece made to stand in one particular place?

Touch—If you could touch this sculpture, how would it feel? What material is it made of? What title would you give the piece?

ASKING QUESTIONS

Above all, involve yourself and your child as much as possible. If you will remember in another chapter, one of the reasons I chose these artists is because they were more accessible than most. Their works are large, easy to see and even touch in some cases. In some cases, security personnel will not allow you touch the work, but I encourage it whenever possible. Look at the work up close, and then stand back. Look at it from the left and right angles. Walk around it. Art very often looks quite different when viewed from different perspectives.

Ask your children what they think. You'll be pleasantly surprised at the stimulating conversations that will ensue. Here are some starter questions to help you. You can also refer to the next page where we give you sample "dialogue starters" for each of these nine artists. Of course, these types of suggestions would work for other artists as well.

1. Do you like this? Why?
2. Assuming you've already shared this book with your child, ask them to identify the artist if they can.
3. Does this art remind you of anything?
4. Is there anything about this piece of art that you don't like? Why?
5. What did the artist use to create this? Oil, acrylics, steel?
6. Would you like to do something like this at home? (Draw, paint, sculpt?)
7. Ask them if it reminds them of anything. Ask them to tell you a story about what they see. This is very important. The creation and telling of a story can be the most powerful tool available to you to enhance your child's experience and memory of a piece of art.
8. After your tour, visit the gift shop and look through their extensive offerings of postcards. Generally, most of the pieces of art displayed in that museum are also available as postcards or prints. This is also a good way to assess what is in the gallery. If you're a little intimidated about finding your way around, purchase the cards of the artists you want to see and show these to the guards and they will direct you there. You can avoid a lot of lost time finding your way around in this manner.
9. On the way home begin to plan your next trip. Make a commitment and do not confine that day's experience to the museum. Look for art in public places. Bring it into your home and discuss it. It doesn't have to be these nine artists

either, go with what you like. Remember, your children have the tendency to like what you like.

WHAT TO WEAR-DRESS CODE

Be practical. Think about your shoes first. You're going to do a fair amount of walking so wear something comfortable like tennies. In some cases, shorts aren't allowed, so ask when you first call. I don't know of any museums that have banned jeans but your best bet overall is to dress casual and comfortably.

SOME FINAL THOUGHTS

Once you've enjoyed your local museum, plan to return frequently. It's also a good idea to become a member of that institution or the American Association of Museums. You'll get freebies; discounts at the gift shops and you'll know that you are supporting a place that honors beauty, excellence and truth. And, perhaps best of all, you and your children will be invited to attend great parties by the museum. You'll meet fascinating new people who will be able to share your newfound excitement.

Also, most museums are now online, so you can now access all the information you'll need for a visit from home. They provide information on their facilities, their collections, featured artists, hours of operation and even directions.

Dropped Bowl and Scattered Slices by Claes Oldenburg

Chapter Six

Basic Art Smarts for Parents

Although most of the work you have been viewing and reading about appears quite simple (as though done by a child), most of them involved a great deal of time and effort. Some of Jackson Pollock's finger paints or drip paintings actually took months to complete; in some cases, years.

This chapter will be devoted to providing you, the parent, some basic knowledge about art in general not only to facilitate your own enjoyment, but so you will be better prepared for some of the extraordinary questions that your children are certain to ask. This will include brief definitions of some of the common words you will hear and see (see glossary for more details), as well as a discussion of techniques and media.

Your children should understand that these artists had a passion for their work. Their work was their "job" and just like mom and dad, they worked at it all day, all month. I think it is important for children to understand that although art is great fun and truly exciting, it also involves a "work ethic" just as their parents' jobs do. Yes, these artists, as most others, loved what they did, but they also had to discipline themselves. Much of their work also involved an on-going education and indeed, a striving for meaning and emotional involvement that at times, could be quite fleeting.

In 1956 artist William de Kooning pointed out "Every so often, a painter has to destroy painting (not a painting, but painting in general), Cezanne did it, and Picasso did it with cubism. Then Jackson Pollock did it. He destroyed our idea of what a picture was. Afterward, there could be new paintings once again."

In 1942, early in Pollock's career, while working on this new ***defining edge*** of painting, another artist, Ms. Lee Krasner, with whom Pollock lived until he died, reported after viewing his work that " . . . in front of a very good painting . . . he asked me, 'Is this a painting?' Not is this a good painting or a bad one, just a painting! The degree of doubt must have been unbelievable at times and yet, at other times, he knew the painter he was."

This chapter is divided into two sections: Why and How.

WHY DO ARTISTS DO WHAT THEY DO?

Generally speaking, the ***creative urge*** (art for art's sake) drives most artists to paint, sculpt, become musicians, actors or writers.

These are the times when artists "create" as an end in itself. They may be inspired, have a vision or just have the need to express themselves. The beaches and fields where he grew up in Long Island, New York inspired Jackson Pollock. When he began painting he tried to communicate, through his paintings, how those landscapes made him feel.

Of course, there are other motivating factors as well. For one, everyone has to make a living and so from the earliest times, artists worked for ***commissions.*** From the 13th century to the present, the church, nobility and the just plain wealthy were the only patrons of the arts. In fact, had it not been for the prolific amount of art commissioned by the church, the entire Renaissance period probably would not have existed. This is why nearly all of the earliest works of art were religious in nature. The church commissioned all of Michelangelo's work.

Today the wealthy are the primary patrons of the arts in all forms as well as various foundations and municipalities.

Jackson Pollock's very first commission was a piece of decorative art for a friend's apartment.

Artists can also derive income from ***contests*** as well as commissions or through gallery sales. And yet other artists such as graphic designers, cartoonists, illustrators, photographers, and even furniture designers and architects derive their incomes either on a freelance basis or by being employed in their given fields.

Regardless of whether emotion lit the flame of inspiration or someone had to pay the rent, most of the time art is still a job.

HOW DO ARTISTS CREATE?

The vehicles and techniques that artists use to create are practically limitless. The Famous Artist known simply as Christo (Javacheff Christo) prefers to create immense works by "draping" entire landscapes in various monolithic curtains or drapes. His work entitled: ***Running Fence***, when viewed from a distance or in a photograph closely resembles the Great Wall of China as it winds its way across a quarter of a mile of Colorado landscape. The entire work is made of sections of orange cloth curtain panels each eight feet wide and twelve feet tall sewn together and suspended by posts and wires. On another occasion, he wrapped an entire bridge in Paris with fabric. And in another instance, he built floating pink plastic skirts to surround eleven islands in Florida. Christo was truly a big thinker.

There are even some works of art that are difficult to categorize, falling somewhere between a play and a sculpture. "Happenings" or ensembles, environments or situations, as they were also referred to, were a form of art indulged in by three of our artists: Oldenburg, Lichtenstein and Grooms among many others. A happening could involve pieces of art such as sculptures or paintings combined with a continual physical action by an artist or artists. It could include displays and playing a musical instrument. Many times, "happenings" were created as a form of demonstration or as a statement for or against some political, religious or cultural situation. When the happening was over, whether that was an hour or a week, everything was dismantled and the artists went home. There was nothing left of the art except for the experience one carried away from it.

Admittedly, Christo's drapings and "happenings" are at the outer reaches of creative options but they do illustrate the unlimited range of mediums and techniques that artists use to express themselves.

For the purposes of keeping our discussion relative to mediums and techniques in this first volume, we will discuss mostly painting, drawing and sculpting, as this is primarily what our nine artists were concerned with.

DRAWING AND PAINTING MEDIUMS AND TECHNIQUES

Drawing and painting most often utilize tools such as pencils, pens, charcoal, and paints such as oils, acrylics and watercolors. In terms of sculpting, an artist most often uses clay, various metals, fabrics and woods. A potter uses clay to create his or her art then sometimes applies a coating of paint or a fixer and then "fires" them in a kiln to dry and harden the pieces.

Traditional sculptors work in clay and then make molds of their creations which are then turned into "bronzes," or they work directly with various metals such as our artists, David Smith and Alexander Calder, using various tools and torches to shape and weld the pieces together, thus eliminating the need for clay or molds.

Most painters use oil, acrylic or watercolor paints to create their work. However, as you have read, Jackson Pollock used car paint, or commercial enamels in much of his work, preferring the consistency and color saturation only achievable through that medium.

With this very general introduction to the various forms of art, I have provided a very detailed glossary at the end of this book. Review these terms before your first art museum visit.

Chapter Seven

Art and Your life

Art is everywhere. Look around you, the lobbies of buildings, in airports, parks, churches, and many public buildings. Art has always been monumentally important to civilization dating back to earliest times—why? There are many reasons and they don't all apply to the art that hangs on walls or marks the city square.

Art as architecture has always been important to civilization from the Egyptian pyramids, to Greece and the Roman Empire, and of course, always in churches, synagogues and mosques to glorify God and to express our devotion. Architecture has always been a way for us to express ourselves in beauty, and to validate our progress as a civilization.

The visual arts as well as architecture also express these same things. In addition, art, from a purely financial viewpoint, helps cities to increase tourism. It gives cities some of their identity, certainly through landmark architecture such as

The Empire State Building in New York City, but also through the major museums and art galleries located there like the Guggenheim in New York, or the new Getty Museum in Los Angeles. Art also expresses something to us about the places we are in and the people who populate them. It makes our environment friendlier, more inviting and relaxing and it can even help orient people by providing directions as landmarks.

Did you know that with all the things there are to do in Italy, the number one tourist attraction is the Pitti Palace in Florence? Young and old alike form lines that go for blocks. Sometimes these people stand in line for hours, even in the summer heat, just to get the chance to walk through and get a glimpse of some of the old masters' paintings and sculptures. These aren't just the wealthy either. They come from all over the world, from every occupation, blue-collar standing next to the blue blood day in and day out. Isn't that amazing? Perhaps not, when you consider the joy and excitement they realize when they are able to see these great works firsthand.

JUST GO FOR IT!

Now that your head is swimming with possibilities, it's time to just go for it. You may be excited and a bit intimidated at the same time. Use the handy directory of museums in the back of this book. Call or go online and find the museum closest to you. Find out when they are open and plan your first trip this weekend. I guarantee you and your children are going to have a ball.

Just remember there is no right or wrong way to enjoy art. In the end, it is only about one thing—**quality time with your child**.

Glossary

Terms, techniques and media

Abstract art: Art which is either completely non-representational, or which converts forms observed in reality into patterns which are read by the spectator primarily as independent relationships, rather than with reference to the original source.

Accidental color: The optical illusion caused by staring at a strongly colored area, then transferring one's gaze to a white or neutral ground. The COMPLEMENTARY of the color one has been gazing at momentarily appears. Thus, if one has been gazing at an area of bright orange, one will see a corresponding patch of green.

Acrylic paint: An emulsion paint using a synthetic medium, acrylic resin, now frequently used by artists as a quick-drying substitute for true oil paint.

"Action": Term used from 1960 to describe a tightly or loosely structured sequence or combination of physical movements, sounds, manipulations of materials, interactions with space and time, etc., not necessarily taking place in one particular setting, and presented as a work of art either directly or through documentation. The "action" is a development of the HAPPENING but is less specifically theatrical. For example, an artist such as Richard Long walking a given number of miles per day along a specified route, and documenting the results with lines drawn on a map and with a camera is first performing, then recording an artistic "action."

Aesthetics: The philosophy of the beauty in art. The term was first used in the mid-18th century by the German philosopher Alexander Gottlieb Baumgarten (1714–62), and was later taken up by Kant in his theory of AESTHETICISM.

Airbrushing: A method of painting by means of a small, finely controllable mechanical paint-sprayer. The method was first used in the GRAPHIC and COMMERCIAL ARTS to achieve a smooth, impersonal finish, and was later adopted by certain practitioners of the FINE ARTS, especially those affiliated with POP ART and SUPER REALISM.

All-over paintings: Paintings, usually ABSTRACT, and dating from the years since the Second World War, which have no central focus or dominate area of interest.

Applied art: Art which is essentially functional, but which is also designed to be aesthetically pleasing (e.g., furniture, metalwork, clocks, textiles, TYPOGRAPHY). See also DECORATIVE ART.

Appliqué: A method of decoration in which a MOTIF is cut from one piece of material and attached, or "applied," to another.

Aquatint: A specialized ETCHING technique, which involves the use of a metal plate coated with a porous resin to create a granulated effect. The parts, which are to appear completely white, are STOPPED OUT with varnish. The plate is immersed in an acid bath, and the microscopic holds in the untreated areas allow the acid to bite into the copper. The resin is then removed, and the process repeated in order to emphasize particular areas, the rest being stopped out, until the plate is etched to the required degree of complexity. The plate, now etched in INTAGLIO, is finally inked and used for printing. Aquatint can also be combined with etched line work.

Art deco: A decorative style named after the great Paris "Exposition Internationale des Arts Décoratifs et Industriels Modernes" held in 1925, but in fact the direct successor to pre-1914 ART NOUVEAU. Even more than Art Nouveau, it emphasized the use of luxurious materials—LACQUER, bronze, ivory, ebony, shagreen—but in contrast to it, stressed very simple, massive forms. Elements taken from the French LOUIS XVI and EMPIRE STYLES were combined with others borrowed from African, Aztec, Chinese art of the Sung period (AD 960–1279) and CUBISM.

"Art for art's sake": Phrase taken over by the English AESTHETIC MOVEMENT from Baudelaire and Gautier and used to imply that their artistic activities needed no moral or social justification.

Art nouveau: An exaggeratedly ASYMMETRICAL decorative style, which spread throughout Europe in the last two decades of the 19th and the first decade of the 20th century. It makes use of undulating forms of all kinds, notably the WHIPLASH CURVE of tendrils or plant stems, but also flames, waves and the flowing hair of stylized female figures. The chief importance of ART NOUVEAU is its rejection of the 19th century HISTORICISM. It is an offshoot of SYMBOLISM on the one hand, and of the ARTS AND CRAFTS MOVEMENT on the other. (The name was taken from that of a shop which opened in Paris as late as 1895 and sold objects of "original" as opposed to PERIOD style.) JUGENDSTIL is the equivalent style in Germany, in France, "Modern Style," and in Italy, "Stile Liberty."

Asymmetrical: Not the same on either side of an axis (but not necessarily out of BALANCE).

Baroque: Term coined by 19th century art historians for the prevailing style in Western European art from 1580 through early 18th century. Their implication since this art was essentially capricious and florid. In fact baroque combined many things: a revolt against MANNERISM and its intellectualism, elitism and emotional coldness, plus a desire to serve the religious impulse of the Counter-Reformation by creating religious types which were accessible to the masses, and also an interest in dynamic movement and theatrical effects. The most typical works of art produced under the baroque combine architecture, sculpture and painting to create a synthesis which has a greater impact than any of these taken separately.

Bauhaus: (Ger. "building house") A design school founded under the leadership of the architect Walter Gropius at Weimar in 1919, which continued and extended the pre-war tradition of the DEUTSCHER WERKBUND. Its aim was to bring together all the arts under the primacy of architecture. After following the EXPRESSIONISTS in emphasizing creative intuition, the Bauhaus soon moved towards the modern world of industry, with teaching methods which stressed the need for a rational, practical approach to design problems, linked to the new doctrines of CONSTRUCTIVISM and NEO-PLASTICISM.

Bevel: The slope or rounding-off of an acute angle in architecture, cabinet-making, etc.

Bezel: 1. The setting for a stone in a piece of jewelry, especially a ring. 2. The metal frame which retains a watch or clock-glass firmly in position. 3. The inner rim on a cover or lid of some kind, especially the lid of a box. 4. Synonym of BEVEL.

Block: 1. A piece of wood, or later metal, ENGRAVED IN RELIEF, which is used to print an image onto a surface, or stamp one into it.

Body: 1. In GOUACHE, white filler used to make the paint opaque. 2. In oil painting, the density of the PIGMENT. 3. In CERAMICS, the type of clay of which a particular ware is made. 4. Also in ceramics, the main part of a vessel, as opposed to the GLAZE and any added features such as the lid, handles, surface decoration, etc.

Body art: A type of ACTION or HAPPENING, in which the artist uses his or her own body as the primary medium of expression. The term has been used from century 1967. Synonym: living sculpture.

Brocade: A fabric with a raised pattern created during the weaving process by using supplementary WEFTS, which are brought to the surface of the cloth when this raised pattern occurs.

Brushwork: The painter's "handwriting," as expressed by the marks made by his brushes on the paint surface.

Bust: A sculpted portrait or representation consisting of the head and part of the shoulders. (The word is sometimes, but wrongly, applied to the head alone.)

Calligraphy: Ornamental writing, done in the West mainly with a pen, in China and Japan with a brush. See also COPPERPLATE, CURSIVE, ITALIC, UNCIALS.

Cameo: A GEMSTONE (or sometimes GLASS, CERAMIC or shell), which has layers of different colors, carved or molded so that the design stands out in RELIEF in one color against the background of the other. The opposite of an INTAGLIO.

Caricature: 1. Strictly, a portrait where the subject's characteristic features are exaggerated for satiric or humorous purposes. 2. Now, more loosely, almost any kind of satiric designs or CARTOON.

Carte-de-visite: 1. Originally, a small portrait photograph used as a supplement to the ordinary visiting card. They were produced in quantity in the 1860s and enthusiastically collected and mounted in albums. 2. A photographic format derived from this, measuring 3-3/4 x 2-1/4 in. (9.5 x 5.7 cm), which was used for both portraits and other subjects, (e.g., landscapes.)

Cartoon: 1. Originally, a full-scale preliminary design for a painting of TAPESTRY. 2. From the 19th century, a CARICATURE or comic drawing (perhaps derived from its use in connection with the controversial designs exhibited in 1843 for the decoration of Barry's new ***Houses of Parliament***).

Cartouche: 1. The oval frame used to enclose the name of an Ancient Egyptian Pharaoh in an inscription. 2. By extension, any ornamental frame.

Casting: The process of making an art object (e.g., a medal, a plaster cast) by running liquid material into a mould. Cashing (as opposed to STRIKING) was the method favored by leading RENAISSANCE medallists such as Pisanello. Types of casting include CIRE PERDUE.

Ceramics: A general term, in use since the 19th century, covering both PORCELAIN and all types of POTTERY.

Chinoiserie: Playful imitation of Chinese art and architecture generally associated with the ROCOCO style in the 18th century Europe.

Classical: 1. Strictly, of the art and architecture of Greek and Roman antiquity, especially Greek work of the 5th and 4th century BC and faithful Roman copies. 2. More generally, of art and architecture, which conform to Greek and Roman models. 3. More generally still, of art which aspires to a state of emotional and physical equilibrium, and which is rationally rather than intuitively constructed.

Clerestory: A row of windows in the upper part of a wall, especially in a church, where they are above the roofs of the flanking AISLES and admit light to the NAVE.

Cloison: 1. In enameling, a cell formed with metal wire or strip, attached to a base and designed to be filled with ENAMEL. 2. In CERAMICS, a cell formed with a ridge of clay on the surface of a piece, and designed to be filled with GLAZE.

Collage: A technique invented by Picasso and Braqué during their analytical CUBIST phase. They began to stick fragments of newspaper and of pre-printed pattern into their compositions, as representatives of the tactile reality, which cubist formal analysis tended to destroy. DADA and SURREALISM as a means of creating irrational conjunctions of "found" imagery later took up collage. (See OBJET TROUVÉ.) However it is used, collage tends to break the unity of the composition and create deliberate spatial disharmonies and incongruities of scale.

Commercial art: Art made not for its own sake but to help sell something, especially in the fields of advertising and technical illustration. The line between commercial art and FINE ART has become increasingly difficult to draw, especially since the rise of POP ART, which makes use of commercial imagery.

Composition: 1. The combination of elements in a painting or other work of art so that they seem satisfactory to the artist. 2. More loosely, a painting, RELIEF or sculptured group, especially if it contains a large number of different elements. 3. See COMPO.

Computer art: Art, mostly drawings and GRAPHICS, produced with the aid of computers. The first computer art appeared in the mid-1950s.

Conceptual art, Concept art: Art of the 1960s, 1970s and 1980s, which is created according to one or more of the following principles: 1. That art consists in the basic idea, which does not have to be embodied in a physical form. 2. That language becomes the basic material of art, and the barrier between art and art theory is breached. 3. That artistic activity becomes an enquiry into the nature of art itself, and any result or embodiment must be regarded simply as an interim demonstration of the general conclusion reached by the artist. Among the artists associated with conceptual art are Lawrence Weiner, Sol LeWitt, Joseph Kosuth and Bruce Nauman, though some of these are also categorized as MINIMALISTS.

Conté: A trade name for synthetic chalks, available in black, sanguine and sepia.

Cool color: A color, which suggests KINAESTHETIC sensations of coolness, such as blue or its associated HUES blue-green and blue-violet. In painting, cool colors appear to recede from the PICTURE-PLANE, and therefore suggest depth.

Copper engraving: 1. A PRINT made from a copper plate engraved with a pointed instrument such as a BURIN. 2. The engraved plate itself.

Crayon: 1. Strictly, PIGMENT and chalk bound with gum so as to form a stick, which can be used for drawing. 2. Now, more loosely, pigment combined with wax to make a stick for drawing.

Crayon manner: An ENGRAVING technique used to reproduce drawings in chalk. It made use of toothed wheels, or roulettes, and similar instruments to imitate the grainy effect of chalk on paper. It was invented in France century 1750, and then widely used in England.

cubism: An art movement which came into being century 1909, led by Picasso and Braque and with its roots in theories put forward by Cézanne. It was an attempt to represent fully and exhaustively on a flat surface, all aspects of what the artist saw in three dimensions.

Analytic cubism showed different aspects of the same object simultaneously, abandoning conventional perspective and using overlapping facets. COLLAGE was a means of importing "raw" reality in order to disrupt the two-dimensionality of this process.

Making use of the insights gained through cubist analysis, *synthetic cubism* translated everything seen into a language of visual signs, providing every object with a coded equivalent, and turning the painting into a parallel reality rather than a reflection of the reality which the painter observed.

Deckle edge: The ragged, irregular edge found on untrimmed handmade paper, which is sometimes imitated by machine-made papers.

Décollage: A work of art based on the destruction or breaking down of materials, e.g., the peeling away of posters. See also COLLAGE.

Découpage: The process of cutting designs out of paper and applying them to a surface to make a COLLAGE.

Design: 1. The general form or COMPOSITION of any building or work of art. 2. In APPLIED ART, the shape given to any object of use and also the way in which it functions.

Die: 1. The DADO of a PEDESTAL. 2. The INTAGLIO stamp used for STRIKING coins and MEDALS or EMBOSSING paper or other materials. 3. A hollow mould for CASTING metal.

Diptych: A pair of PANELS or leaves hinged together.

Donor: A person responsible for commissioning a painting – typically a late medieval altarpiece – that is portrayed within the painting itself (a donor portrait), and often accompanied by a patron saint.

Drawing: 1. A representation by means of lines. 2. The arrangement of lines, which determine a particular FORM. Something is said to be "out of drawing" when the representation in two dimensions does not reconstitute itself, in the spectator's eye and mind, into a convincing three-dimensional form.

Dry brush painting: In oils or watercolor, the very scanty use of PIGMENT on a textured surface. The paint clings to the raised parts of the surface only.

Drying oils: Fatty oils of vegetable origin which are of major importance in oil painting as a MEDIUM for PIGMENT, because they harden into a solid, transparent substance on exposure to air. They also serve as a binder, fixing the pigment to the GROUND. The chief drying oils are linseed, walnut and poppy. Synonym: fixed oils.

Earth colors: Pigments such as brown or yellow, which occur naturally in earth or clay and are usually metallic oxides. Chemically, they are the most stable of all pigments and therefore the least subject to change in the aging process.

Eclectic: (Used of artistic styles.) Consisting of an amalgam of elements from other styles. The term originated in Greek philosophy where it was applied to philosophers who tired to take the best from several conflicting schools.

Edition: All the copies of a PRINT or book made from a single printing.

Electroplating: A process, patented, by G.R. Elkington in 1840, which makes use of electrolysis to coat a base metal, usually nickel, with a thin layer of silver.

Embossing: Any process (e.g., CASTING, CHASING, stamping, carving or molding) designed to make a pattern or FIGURATIVE composition stand out in RELIEF. Sometimes also used as a synonym for REPOUSSÉ.

Embroidery: A method of decorating textiles with stitched threads in different patterns. (As opposed to TAPESTRY where the design is woven into the fabric.)

Engraving: 1. The process of making a design on a hard surface by inscribing it with a point. 2. By extension, an INTAGLIO PRINT made by cutting into the printing surface with a point. See also ETCHING, COPPER ENGRAVING, WOOD ENGRAVING. (CAMERA OBSCURA, SUBLIME.)

Etching: 1. The process of making a design on a metal PLATE by means of the action of acid. The design is scratched through an acid-resistant coating, or etching-ground, with a needle, exposing these parts of the metal beneath. The plate is then immersed in an acid bath, where the acid bites into the lines of the design. The longer the plate is left, the deeper the lines become. Repeated bitings may be used to emphasize certain parts of the design, the rest being protected (topped out) with varnish. This technique is often combined with ENGRAVING. 2. A PRINT produced by these methods.

expressionism: 1. A term first popularized by the German art critic Herwarth Walden, publisher of the Berlin AVANT-GARDE review *Der Sturm* (1910-32), to characterize all the modern art opposed to IMPRESSIONISM. 2. Later, art in which the forms arise, not directly from observed reality, but from subjective reactions to reality. 3. Today, any art in which conventional ideas of REALISM and PROPORTION seem to have been overridden by the artist's emotion with resultant distortions of shape and color.

Face painting: Archaic English term for portrait painting, dating from the 16th century, when painters were still regarded as artisans.

Firing: Heating CERAMIC, GLASS or ENAMEL objects in a kiln, either to harden them, to fuse the components, or to fuse GLAZE or enamel to a ceramic BODY or metal PLAQUE.

Fixative: A colorless solution sprayed onto designs made in impermanent materials such as chalk, pastel or charcoal to fix them in place and prevent smudging.

Formalism: Art, and critical writing about art, which place the emphasis on the analysis of FORM and the use of formal elements rather than on CONTENT. Often used as a term of abuse by communist critics, who regard it as the inverse and opponent of SOCIALIST REALISM.

Format: The size and proportions of a piece of paper, canvas, or book page.

Free form: Irregular or asymmetrical shapes, especially curvilinear ones, in painting, sculpture or decorative objects.

Fresco: (It. "fresh") True fresco (*buon alfresco,* as distinct from *fresco* SECCO) is painting done with mineral or earth PIGMENTS upon wet lime or gypsum PLASTER. (Vegetable pigments cannot be used as they are attacked by the lime.) The pigments are suspended in water, and unite with the plaster as they dry. The basis is a ROUGHCAST wall, covered with a layer of plaster (the *arricciato*), on which the composition (the *sinopia*) is sketched out in charcoal and SINOPIA. Only wet plaster (the *intonaco*) is then applied for a day's work, any subsequent retouching being done in *fresco secco.*

Functionalism: The theory that "form follows function," first enunciated by the American architect Louis Sullivan at the end of the 19th century but anticipated by the empiricist philosophy of the 18th century According to this theory, only objects, which both function well and use material with economy, are admissible in the domestic environment.

Futurism: An art movement founded in 1909 by the Italian writer F.T. Marinetti. It was originally purely literary, aiming to break the bonds of grammar, syntax and logic in a celebration of the sensations and sounds of the technological world of the future. Museum art was spurned as "passéist," and the coming war eagerly welcomed. In the futurist painting and sculpture of Giacomo Balla, ***Umberto Boccioni*** and others, the emphasis was on giving an impression of speed, on SIMULTANEITY and on the interpenetration of planes. Futurism was skillfully publicized in a series of manifestos and in public performances in which the audience was goaded into uproar. It influenced CUBO-FUTURISM, DADA, SUPREMATISM, and VORTICISM. The JACK OF DIAMONDS group was the focus of the movement in Russia.

Gallery: 1. In ecclesiastical architecture, the upper storey over a side AISLE, open to the body of the church but not to the exterior. Often wrongly called a TRIFORIUM. 2. (Or "long gallery") A long narrow room in a grand private house used for recreation and exercise, particularly in bad weather. 3. A place where paintings and other works of art are displayed. 4. An upper storey open on one side to the main interior space, especially in a place of public resort, such as a theatre. 5. In churches and secular buildings, a kind of exterior corridor, communicating through an ARCADE or COLONNADE with the open air. Synonym: loggia. 6. A narrow passage running along the side of a larger room or interior space, with openings into it.

Gesso: (It. "gypsum") A mixture of gypsum and SIZE, used both as a GROUND for TEMPERA, for some types of oil painting and gliding, and for modeled decoration on furniture and picture-frames (*gesso rilievo*). See also COMPO.

Glaze: 1. In CERAMICS, a VITREOUS coating designed to make the BODY impervious to water, and also serving as decoration. 2. In painting, a transparent layer of paint applied over another layer, or over a GROUND, of a different color in order to modify it. 3. To fill a window with panes of GLASS.

Gothic: A word now used to describe all medieval art from the end of the ROMANESQUE period (mid-12th century) to the beginning of the RENAISSANCE (early 15th century), but applied especially to architecture using pointed arches, rib VAULTS, FLYER BUTTRESSES, etc. The classification of Gothic traditionally used in England runs from EARLY ENGLISH through DECORATED, to PERPENDICULAR and is based on the development of window forms. The term was coined by Renaissance architects in order to deride their immediate predecessors as "Goths" or barbarians.

Gouache: (Fr. "wash") Painting in opaque WATERCOLORS. The PIGMENTS have a gum BINDER, and the FILLER is invariably some form of opaque white (such as clay or barite), which gives a typical "chalky" look even to dark HUES. Synonyms: poster paint, body color.

Graphic art: A form of artistic expression where the statement is made, usually on paper, through emphasis on lines, marks or printed letters rather than on color. It includes everything from drawing, through PRINT-making of all kinds, to TYPOGRAPHY.

Ground: 1. A surface specially prepared for painting, perhaps with GESSO or a layer of paint of even TONE. An absorbent ground is one that contains no oil and therefore absorbs the oil from the paint, which becomes matt and dries quickly. 2. More loosely, the SUPPORT on which a painting or drawing is executed—canvas, paper or PLASTER. 3. A subordinate background in a painting. See FIGURE-GROUND RELATIONSHIP. 4. In the decorative arts, the basic material on which a representation, ornament or pattern is superimposed. For example, in ENAMELLING, the ground is usually of metal, and in CERAMICS, it is the BODY of the vessel used as a background for decoration. 5. In ETCHING, the acid-resistant coating on the metal plate through which the needle is drawn.

Happening: An art event typical of the 1960s and 1970s which synthesized both planned and improvised theatrical activity, the visual arts and found materials (see OBJET TROUVÉ). Audience participation was also often invited. The form evolved century 1957–59 in New York as an extension into time and space of the free improvisation of ABSTRACT EXPRESSIONISM and was an important stage in the evolution of POP ART. The composer John Cage and his theories concerning the use of chance also influenced its emergence. The most striking difference between the happening and more conventional kinds of theatre is the lack of narrative. See also ACTION.

High Renaissance: The culminating phase of RENAISSANCE art century 1495–1520, typified by the work of Raphael, Michelangelo and Leonardo da Vinci.

Horizon-line: In linear PERSPECTIVE,* the line where sky and earth seem to meet. It is on this line that the VANISHING POINT is located.

Icon: A painting by a Greek or Russian Orthodox believer on PANEL, generally of a religious subject strictly prescribed by tradition, and using an equally strict prescribed pattern of representation. An authentic icon can be of any age from the 6th century AD to the present day.

Illusionism: The use of pictorial devices, chief among them PERSPECTIVE and FORESHORTENING, so as to persuade the spectator that what he or she sees is real.

Impressionism: French 19th century art movement, which tried to use contemporary scientific research into the physics of color (including work carried out by Eugène Chevreul) to achieve a more exact representation of color and TONE. The majority of the impressionists applied paint in small touches of pure color rather than broader, blended strokes, thus making pictures, which seemed dazzlingly brighter than those of contemporary SALON artists. They also believed in painting out of doors, and in trying to catch a particular fleeting impression of color and light rather than making a synthesis in the studio. The painters connected with the movement came together just before the Franco-Prussian War of 1870–71. The First impressionist exhibition was held in 1874, and included work by Monet, Renoir, Sisley, Pissarro, Cézanne, Degas, Guillaumin, Boudin and Berthe Morisot.

Intaglio: 1. A hollow-cut design, i.e., the opposite of RELIEF. An intaglio is often used as a MATRIX from which a relief can be made for a coin, MEDAL or sealing. Synonym: cavo rilievo. 2. A hollow-cut GEMSTONE. See also CAMEO.

Kinetic art: Art which incorporates an element of mechanical or random movement, or which gives the illusion of movement by the use of optical techniques (OP ART). It was first used by the CONSTRUCTIVISTS in the early 20th century and was further popularized by Alexander Calder with his MOBILES in the 1930s, but came to full prominence in the 1950s.

Lacquer: An extremely hard waterproof varnish, which originated in the Far East. One kind is made from the sap of the *Rhus vernicifera* tree, which polymerizes on exposure to air. For use as lacquer, it needs only to be strained and heated to reduce the volume of liquid. It can be built up in layers, and is then hard enough to be carved. (COROMANDEL LACQUER is made by this method.) Another kind (shellac) is made by extracting the secretion of the lac insect, *Coccus lacca,* by immersing the creature in boiling water. This secretion, called lac, is then melted into think flakes and dissolved in alcohol so that it can be used as lacquer. See also JAPANNED WORK, VERNIS MARTIN.

Landscape format: A painting, drawing, etc., which is wider than it is high (i.e., the opposite of PORTRAIT FORMAT). So called because most representations of landscape have this shape.

Layout: An annotated diagram showing the positioning of typographical matter, and illustrations if any, on the page. (See also ARTWORK.)

Lithograph: A PRINT made by drawing on fine-grained porous limestone or on a zinc plate with greasy material, then wetting the stone or plate and applying greasy ink, which will adhere only to the drawn lines. Dampened paper is applied to the stone and is rubbed over with a special press to make the final print. (PYLON)

Mannerism: (Fr. It. *maniera,* "style") 1. Term coined in the 20th century to describe the European art of the period 1515–1610. It is typified by stylistic trickery and a liking for bizarre effects. CONTRAPPOSTO and the extreme elongation of the figure occur frequently in both painting and sculpture. Mannerist art conveys a sense of neurotic disquiet, and tends to concentrate on style rather than content, while the content itself is often complicated and esoteric. In the DECORATIVE ARTS, there is a taste for virtuosity and the unexpected. Outside Italy, mannerism was nearly always a court style, and everywhere it addressed the few rather than the many. 2. (With a small "m") Any art of any period with some of the characteristics described above, e.g., the AMMAN art of Ancient Egypt.

Masterpiece: Under the medieval GUILD system, the obligatory test-piece by which an apprentice showed that he had qualified as a master of his craft. Later the word was applied to any work of preeminent merit.

Medium: 1. The liquid in which PIGMENT is suspended in any kind of painting. Thus, linseed oil is the medium most often used in oil painting. 2. The physical substance chosen as a vehicle of expression by any visual artist. Thus, marble is a medium in sculpture.

Mezzotint: (It. "half tint") A method of ENGRAVING in which the artist works from dark to light. The whole GROUND is first of all covered with a regular fine scratching made by using a rocking tool called a cradle. This takes the ink and appears as a black background. The design is burnished onto it, does not take the ink and therefore appears in white.

Minimal art: Term coined in the 1960s to describe art, which abandons all pretensions at either expressiveness or illusion. It is generally three-dimensional, and either shaped by chance (e.g., a heap of sand) or made up of simple geometrical forms, often used repetitively. Carl André's sculptures made of bricks are the most famous example of the latter. See also GESTALT.

Mixed media: 1. Art of the 20th century, which combines different types of physical material. 2. Art, which draws on several disciplines, for example music, movement and environmental sculpture. In this sense, synonymous with intermedia and multimedia.

Mobile: A complex work of art, constructed of moving parts, hanging or standing, which can be either wind-driven or mechanically powered. Its form continually changes, as each shift creates a new set of relationships. The term itself was coined by Marcel Duchamp in 1932, to describe Alexander Calder's works.

Modeling: 1. The representation of three-dimensional forms in two dimensions so that they appear solid. 2. The use of malleable material (e.g., wax or clay) to create a form, which is three-dimensional.

Modernism, Modern movement: General name given to the succession of AVANT-GARDE styles in art and architecture, which have dominated Western culture almost throughout the 20th century.

Monolith: A sculpture, monument or architectural member (e.g., a pillar) made from a single block of stone.

Motif: 1. A distinct or separable element in the design of a painting, sculptures, building or pattern. 2. The subject of a painting.

Naturalism: 1. An artistic tendency prevailing throughout Europe in the second half of the 19th century, which led painters to become more and more interested in the depiction of the trivia of ordinary life. It also had a parallel in literature (e.g., in the ***Novels of Zola*** and the ***Goncourts***.) Naturalism influenced artists otherwise as different from one another as Degas, Adolf von Menzel and Ilya Repin. 2. Any art dependent on suggestions taken from nature rather than on intellectual theory. Often confused with REALISM.

Negative: 1. A photographic PLATE or film with tonal and (where present) color values reversed, which produce a POSITIVE image when light is passed through it to fall on sensitized paper. 2. An INTAGLIO stamp or mould. 3. A negative image is one where the effect of RELIEF or color seems to have been reversed, and to have become the opposite of what it is in reality.

Neo-classicism: The style of decoration, based on Ancient Greek and Roman examples, which made its appearance in the 1750s as a reaction to the capricious excesses of the ROCOCO, and which was fully established by the 1770s. It is characterized by a preference for the linear and the symmetrical, and for flatness rather than PLASTICITY.

Neo-expressionism: Violent FIGURATIVE art, largely a revival of early 20th century. German EXPRESSIONIST forms, which manifested itself in the U.S., Italy and (especially) West Germany during the late 1970s. Among the artists associated with the tendency were Georg Baselitz, Rainer Fetting and Anselm Kiefer (German), Julian Schnabel (American) and Sandro Chia (Italian). In the U.S., it is termed "Bad Painting," in Italy "TRANSAVANGUARDIA," and in Germany, the artists are known as "Neue Wilden" ("New Wild Ones").

Neo-impressionism: An offshoot of IMPRESSIONISM, which subjected impressionist techniques to rigorous intellectual analysis. Seurat was its leader, and Signac and (for a while) Camille Pissarro were among its chief adherents. It was characterized by the use of DIVISIONISM and by strictly formal compositions.

Neo-plasticism: Theory of art propounded by Mondrian, which influenced his painting, and that of disciples such as Theo Van Doesburg, between 1912 and 1920. Its precepts were that art was to be entirely ABSTRACT, that only right angles in the horizontal and vertical positions were to be used, and that the colors were to be simple PRIMARIES, supplemented with white, black and grey.

Neo-romanticism: Strongly theatrical, romantic style of painting of the 1930s and 1940s, influenced by SURREALISM. Among the artists connected with the movement were the Frenchman, Christian Bérard, the American, Eugene Berman, and the Englishman, John Piper.

New York School: The innovative, New-York-based ABSTRACT painting, which began to develop during the 1940s. It included ABSTRACT EXPRESSIONISM, but also artists only very loosely related to this movement. Among its principal members were Jackson Pollock, Mark Rothko and Adolph Gottlieb.

Objet d'art: A piece of decorative art of small size and (generally) exquisite finish.

Op art: An ABSTRACT art movement of the 1960s concerned with the exploration of various optical effects achieved by retinal stimulation. Typical works were produced by Bridget Riley, Solo and Victor Vasarely. See also KINETIC ART, MOIRÉ.

Painterly: (Fr. Ger. *malerisch*) Representing form, not by means of outline, but by the mingling of light and shade, rendered as indeterminate patches of color. The Swiss art historian Heinrich Wölfflin first used the word in this sense in 1915.

Panorama: A circular painting on the scale of life, which surrounds the spectator, so that he or she has the impression of looking at a real view. Panoramas were popular entertainment in the late 18th and early 19th century. See also DIORAMA.

Papier mache: Pulped paper, usually combined with glue, chalk and sometimes sand. It can be shaped by molding and then baking, and was used extensively in the 18th and 19th century for small articles of furniture and decorative objects.

Papyrus: A species of rush (reed). The stem was flattened and used by the Ancient Egyptians as a surface to write on, and the external appearance of the plant inspired the architectural ornament of some of their buildings, e.g., papyrus CAPITAL.

Pastel: Dry PIGMENT bound with gum and used in stick form for drawing. A fixative is used to make it adhere to the GROUND.

Pastiche: A work of art using a borrowed style and usually made up of borrowed elements, but not necessarily a direct copy. A pastiche often verges on conscious or unconscious CARICATURE, through its exaggeration of what seems most typical in the original model.

Pastoral: A landscape painting which represents the countryside as a sort of Arcadia peopled with demi-gods, nymphs, satyrs, shepherds and shepherdesses. See also F TE CHAMP TRE.

Patina: 1. Strictly, the colored (usually green or brown) incrustation on bronze caused by oxidation. 2. By extension, any pleasing alteration of surface color or texture due to age, use or exposure.

Pencil: 1. In the 18th century an artist's brush. Hence "pencilling" meant brushwork. 2. In modern usage, a drawing or writing instrument generally consisting of a stick of graphite or chalk encased in either wood or metal.

Performance art: Art of the 1960s and later which is closely linked to the performing arts—mime, dance and theatre—and which is presented as an ephemeral event before an audience. Comprises ACTIONS, BODY ART and "happenings."

Period: (Used adjectivally of architecture and the decorative arts.) Of a certain period in the past.

Perspective: The method of representing a three-dimensional object, or a particular volume of space, on a flat or nearly flat surface.

Atmospheric perspective. A means of representing distance and recession in a painting, based on the way the atmosphere affects the human eye. Outlines become less precise, small details are lost, HUES become noticeably more blue, colors in general become paler, color contrasts are less pronounced. These effects had already been observed by FRESCO painters of the Roman period but on the whole are most typical of NATURALISTIC European landscape painting from the 16th century onwards. There is also an attempt at atmospheric perspective in Chinese and Japanese ink painting.

Centralized perspective. Linear perspective in which the eye is drawn towards a single VANISHING POINT in the centre of the composition, usually on the horizon-line. Synonym: one-point perspective.

Linear perspective uses real or suggested lines converging on a vanishing point or points on the horizon or at eye-level, and linking receding plans as they do so.

One-point perspective. Synonym of centralized perspective.

Photomontage: A pictorial composition made by covering a sheet of paper or card with overlapping photographs or fragments of photographs. See also MONTAGE.

Pictograph: A highly simplified symbol of an object or action.

Picture-plane: The imaginary plane represented by the physical surface (canvas, paper, etc.) of a painting.

Pietà: (It. "pity") A representation of the dead Christ lying in the lap of the mourning Virgin. It originated as a type in Germany in the 14th century.

Pigment: 1. The coloring agent in paint or dye. 2. The same coloring agent isolated in dry form, usually as a powder.

Piqué work: (Fr. *piqué*, "pitted") 1. Material, usually tortoiseshell or ivory, ornamented with an INLAY of minute points of gold. 2. A kind of fine embroidery, made with very short stitches, which appear as points of color.

Plaster: Malleable material which hardens when dry and is made from a wide variety of materials, most of the mixtures containing limestone, sand and water, with hair as a strengthener. It is used to coat walls, externally or internally (sometimes as a GROUND for FRESCO), for molded and carved architectural ornament (see also STUCCO), for molded copies of sculpture (PLASTER OF PARIS), and (usually as a basis for gilding) on a wooden foundation for picture frames and ornamental furniture. See also COMPO, GESSO, STUCCO, and PLASTER OF PARIS.

Pointing: 1. A mechanical process for enlarging a small model, or BOZZETTO, into a full-sized sculpture by measuring off from a series of "points" marked on the original to similar points on the copy (i.e., a three-dimensional equivalent of SQUARING FOR TRANSFER). 2. The process of raking out joints in building mortar and pressing in new mortar to create a smooth surface.

Pop art: Art, which makes use of the imagery of consumerism and mass culture (e.g., comic strips, pin-ups and packaging) with a finely balanced mixture of irony and celebration. Pop art began in the 1950s with various investigations into the nature of urban popular culture, notably by members of the Independent Group at the ICA (Institute of Contemporary Arts) in London. It blossomed in 1960 as a major style, having taken on board certain ideas, which had their roots in DADA. It finally affected not only FINE ART but also many aspects of DECORATIVE ART. Pop artists in the U.S. included Roy Lichtenstein, James Rosenquist and Claes Oldenburg, and in Britain Richard Hamilton, Allen Jones and Peter Phillips.

Poster paint: Synonym of GOUACHE.

Post-impressionism: General term for the work of the major artists of Western Europe, not closely linked stylistically, who developed away from IMPRESSIONISM. Chief among them were Cézanne, Gauguin, Van Gogh and Toulouse-Lautrec. The term was first used century 1914 by the English critic and artist Roger Fry.

Post-modern: Term used to describe the attempt to modify and extend the tradition of MODERNISM in 20th century. Architecture with borrowings from the CLASSICAL tradition, from vernacular building methods and from commercial styles. Many of these references are used ironically. The word was first used in an architectural context by Joseph Hudnut in 1949, but given wider circulation by Charles Jencks and his associates and allies from 1975, and much elaborated upon in Jencks' book, *The Language of Post Modern Architecture* (1977).

Post-painterly abstraction: Term coined by the American art critic Clement Greenberg in 1964 to describe the work of American artists such as Morris Louis, Kenneth Noland, Jules Olitski and Ellsworth Kelly, who were then using large fields of pure color, unmodulated by brushwork. Such work is also sometimes described as COLOR-FIELD PAINTING, in spite of the fact that this term also includes an earlier generation of artists such as Yves Klein, Ad Reinhardt and Barnett Newman. The term is thus dependent not merely on the appearance of the work, but on the identity of the artists Greenberg associated with it.

Pottery: All wares made of fired clay except PORCELAIN (e.g., EARTHENWARE and STONEWARE.)

Priming: Material, usually neutral-colored paint, applied to a canvas or wooden panel to protect and seal it before the final painting.

Primitivism: 1. Any art, which deliberately adopts PRIMITIVE characteristics. 2. A Russian art movement of century 1905–20 which combined influences from Russian FOLK ART with ideas borrowed from CUBISM and FUTURISM. Among its adherents were Larionov, Goncharova, and the young Malevich. (DONKEY'S TAIL.)

Process Art: Art of the mid 1960s and 1970s where the process of creation becomes the subject matter. The spectators are invited to reconstruct what has been done, through the evidence placed before them. Among the artists associated with the term are Richard Serra, Robert Morris and Lawrence Weiner.

Proof: A trial pull, or proof impression, of an ETCHING or ENGRAVING, made so that the artist can see whether the composition needs to be revised, or whether it can be left as it is. A "touched proof" is one with alterations made by hand.

Purism: Art movement founded in 1915 by the painters Amédée Ozenfant and Charles Edouard Jeanneret (better known as an architect under his pseudonym Le Corbusier). They published a manifesto entitled *Après le cubisme* ("After cubism") in 1918. Purism was an attempt to reform the later, more decorative, phase of CUBISM by returning to simple, extremely generalized basic forms.

Realism: 1. Art, which aims to reproduce reality exactly. 2. (With a capital R) A phase of 19th century French art. Rejecting the idealistic tendencies of ROMANTICISM, leading French artists of the mid century such as Courbet concentrated on reproducing what was immediately accessible to them, in terms of both social and sensory experience. Their bent towards detailed, accurate, sober representation was encouraged by the impact of photograph. See also PEINTRES DE LA RÉALITÉ, LES.

Reflected color: A change in HUE brought about when one color is reflected onto another.

Regionalism: The work of a small group of North American artists of the 1930s and 1940s who concentrated on rural Midwestern subject matter and rejected most forms of European influence. Leading members of the group were Thomas Hart Benton, Grant Wood (see AMERICAN GOTHIC) and John Steuart Curry. Many of the artists concerned were closely connected with the WPA.

Relief: 1. A composition or design made so that all or part projects from a flat surface. 2. The impression or illusion of three dimensions given by a painting.

Renaissance: The classically inspired revival of European arts and letters, which began in Italy in the 14th century Intellectually it was inspired by the ideas of humanist scholars, and in the visual arts, its progress was marked by greater and greater command of anatomy and of the techniques of linear and atmospheric PERSPECTIVE, as well as by increasingly secular subject-matter, with themes taken from classical legend and history as well as from religion. The Renaissance in Italy lasted from the 14th century until about 1580 (thus incorporating early MANNERISM), but the High Renaissance lasted only from century 1480 to century 1527 (the Sack of Rome), and was dominated by Leonardo, Raphael, and Michelangelo in his earlier phases. Its influence was also felt throughout Europe, and the paintings of Albrecht Dürer and of the FONTAINEBLEAU SCHOOL can also be described as Renaissance art.

Rendering: A waterproof coating, generally PLASTER or cement, on a wall exposed to the weather.

Replica: 1. Strictly, an exact copy of a painting or sculpture done by the artist who created the original. 2. More loosely, one of two versions of a painting when it is not known which is the original. 3. An object exactly reproducing another object, usually one by a different hand.

Reproduction: 1. A copy of a work of art, especially one made by mechanical means (e.g., CASTING, photography). 2. (Of furniture, etc. Also used adjectivally.) A more or less accurate copy of an earlier piece in PERIOD style.

Resist: Wax or varnish used to cover areas of cloth, POTTERY or an ETCHING plate, which are to be left clear of dye, LUSTRE or acid. (In the latter case, refers to both the "ground" and the "stopping-out varnish.")

Rococo: (Fr., *rocaille*) A lighter and more playful version of the BAROQUE, associated with the reign of Louis XV in France, and typified by asymmetry, the use of florid S-CURVES and c-scrolls, and of naturalistic motifs derived from rocks, shells and plants. The Rococo is more immediately identifiable in the DECORATIVE ARTS than it is in architecture or painting. The term did not come into general use until the 1830s, and long retained a pejorative implication.

Sand blasting: A technique for decorating glass, gold or concrete, or for cleaning stone, metal, etc., by directing a stream of sand, crushed flint or iron filings at the surface under pressure. Those parts to be left plain are protected by a stencil or some form of RESIST. The method was first used (for decorating glass) in the U.S. in 1870.

Saturation: The brilliance of a color — i.e., the extent to which a particular red, for example, impresses the viewer by its redness.

Scale: Proportion or measurement. Something drawn "one-third scale" is drawn one third the size of the original.

School: A group of artists working under the influence of a single master, or possessing a similarity because they come from the same region or practice the same local style.

Sculpture: 1. Any work of art carried out in three dimensions. 2. With the advent of CONCEPTUAL ART in the 1970s, the word also began to be used for a wide variety of AVANT-GARDE works of art, some consisting only of a series of written statements (e.g. by Lawrence Weiner), and others using the dimension of time as well as space. When the British artist Richard Long made one of his planned walks across country, and recorded what he had done on a map, this ACTION was also labeled "sculpture." The word has thus become a label for almost any form of art activity other than painting.

Serigraphy: A PRINT-making technique based on STENCILLING. Ink or paint is brushed through a fine screen made of silk, and masks are used to produce the design. These can be made of paper, or from VARNISH applied to the silk itself. Synonym: silk-screen printing. (POP ART)

Significant form: A term coined by the English art critic Clive Bell in 1913 to describe what seemed to him the essence of true works of art; the forms, and relationships of forms, which they contain. According to this doctrine FORM itself is the true CONTENT of the work of art, and other kinds of content (e.g. narrative and symbolic elements) are secondary.

Silhouette: 1. A PROFILE portrait cut out of black paper or painted in solid black. Originally made from a tracing of the shadow cast by a bright light and named after Etienne de Silhouette, an 18th century French politician. 2. By extension, any object or scene shown in black with no interior detail.

Sketch: A rough preliminary version of a composition.

Slip: A creamy dilution of clay, often in a different color to the BODY of the vessel, which is used to coat it (often making it waterproof), to decorate it or to join parts together. See also SGRAFFITO, ENGOBE.

Soak-stain technique: A method of painting which produces soft stains or blots of color through the use of heavily diluted paint or unsized canvas (see SIZE). The technique is typical of POST-PAINTERLY ABSTRACTION, and especially of the work of Morris Louis.

Soft sculpture: Sculpture made of "soft" materials (canvas, rope, vinyl, latex, etc.), which take on shapes in response to gravity. It began to be made in the 1960s by POP artists such as Claes Oldenburg, but has since developed more widely in the hands of

MINIMAL and PROCESS artists such as Robert Morris.

Stylus: (Lat.) Any pointed implement used for making a lightly indented mark or scratch. See DIAMOND-POINT ENGRAVING.

Surrealism: (Fr. *surréel,* "transcending the real") Term coined by Guillaume Apollinaire in 1917, but now used for a movement founded by André Breton in 1924, which absorbed the French DADA movement and made positive claims for such methods and processes (defiance of logic, shock tactics) which Dada had used merely as a negation of conventional art. Influenced by Freud, it claimed to liberate the riches of the unconscious through the "primacy of dream" and the suspension of conscious control (AUTOMATISM). Initially literary, it found artistic expression in COLLAGE and FROTTAGE (Max Ernst), in so-called veristic surrealism (fantastic subjects painted in obsessive detail by artists such as Salvador Dalí and Yves Tanguy) and through a freehand ABSTRACTION based on automatism (André Masson), which influenced ABSTRACT EXPRESSIONISM.

Symbolism: An influential movement, both in European literature and in the visual arts, from 1885 to 1910. Symbolism rejected objectivity in favor of the subjective, and turned away from the direct representation of reality in favor of a synthesis of many different aspects of it, aiming to suggest ideas by means of ambiguous yet powerful symbols. It combined religious mysticism with an interest in the perverse and the erotic, an interest in what seemed "primitive" with a sophisticated cult of decadence. Among the artists associated with the movement were Odilon Redon, Gustave Moreau and Puvis de Chavannes in France, Fernand Khnopff in Belgium, Jan Toorop in Holland, Ferdinand Hodler in Switzerland, Gustav Klimt in Austria, and Giovanni Segantini in Italy. See also NABIS, ROSICRUCIANS, and SYNTHETISM.

Systemic painting: A form of ABSTRACT painting which expresses a logical system of some sort, e.g. the repetition and progressive variation of a single MOTIF, either on one canvas or on a series of related canvases.

Tempera: (It., Fr., Lat. *temperare,* "to mix in due proportion") An EMULSION used as a MEDIUM for PIGMENT. Traditionally, tempera is made with whole eggs or egg-yolk, but milk, various kinds of glue or gum, or even dandelion juice or the sap of the fig tree can be used. The medium is particularly associated with Italian painters of the 14th and 15th century, who used it both for FRESCO and PANEL PAINTINGS. (CASSONE)

Terracotta: (It. "baked earth") 1. Fired clay with no GLAZE, used for building, architectural ornament and sculpture. (Etruscan art,* bas-RELIEF.*) 2. A color resembling fired clay.

Terrazzo: A mixture of marble chips and cement, used for flooring. It is laid *in situ,* ground smooth and then polished.

Texture: 1. In art and architecture, the nature of the surface of a painting, sculpture, building, etc. 2. By extension, the general material qualities of a work of art, such as the rhythm of the brush-strokes in a loosely handled painting (e.g. in the work of Velásquez).

Throwing: The process of making a CERAMIC object on a potter's wheel.

Tint: The dominant color in an admixture of colors or in a mixture of color and white, e.g. "a bluish tint" or "a bluish white."

Tintype: A photograph on a small PLATE of tinned iron, produced by using a variant of the collodion WET PLATE PROCESS that gives a positive rather than a negative image. The plates were cheaper and easier to handle than glass negatives or positives, and, if used for portrait photography, the resulting PRINT could be handed to the sitter within a few minutes of the exposure being made. The process was invented in 1853 by the Frenchman, Adolphe Alexandre Martin, and became popular in the U.S. from 1860. Synonym: ferrotype.

Tonal values: The relative lightness or darkness of the various parts of a painting, irrespective of color. The contrasts so produced are particularly extreme in CHIAROSCURO.

Tone: 1. The prevailing HUE in a picture. 2. Its comparative brightness or dullness.

Toning: In oil painting, the process of unifying the monochrome under painting by adding a GLAZE or by SCUMBLING to get rid of extreme contrasts of light and dark before adding LOCAL COLOR.

Tooth: The slight roughness of canvas or other SUPPORT, which enables paint to cling to it more firmly.

Toys: Term used in the 18th century for small ornamental articles in a variety of materials including PORCELAIN and silver. Birmingham silversmiths specializing in small items such as vinaigrettes (miniature boxes in precious metal containing scented sponges) were known as "toy-makers."

Triptych: A picture made up of three panels, the two outer ones usually hinged so that they fold like doors in front of the main scene. See also DIPTYCH, POLYPTYCH.

Typeface: Any of the thousands of letterforms, often very subtly differentiated, that are used in printing. Each typeface is available in a number of sizes; this book, for example, is set in 9 point Bembo. For the families of typefaces in the Roman alphabet, see BLACK LETTER, FRAKTUR, LETTRE BÂTARDE, ROMAN, ITALIC, SANS SERIF, SCHWABACHER.

Under glaze: Painted decoration on CERAMIC, applied before the GLAZE, and permanently fixed when the glaze is fired.

Vanishing point: In PERSPECTIVE, the point towards which a set of lines, which are in reality parallel to each other, seem to converge. See also FOCAL POINT. (RENAISSANCE)

Varnish: Resin dissolved in a MEDIUM and used either as a protective coating (which can be tinted), or sometimes as a VEHICLE for PIGMENT, and therefore as a kind of paint.

Vehicle: The MEDIUM, or the combination of MEDIUM plus BINDER, which carries PIGMENTS in suspension, and enables them to be applied and adhere to a surface. In distemper, the MEDIUM is water and the BINDER is glue — together they make SIZE, which is the VEHICLE.

Veneer: Extremely thin sheets of wood, often chosen for their ornamental figure, used to cover the surface of furniture constructed of coarser and cheaper wood. Veneers can also be made of such materials as ivory, tortoiseshell and brass. See also BOULLE MARQUETRY, MARQUETRY, PARQUETRY.

Video art: Television and video-recording technology used in works of art (e.g. by Nam June Paik).

Vignette: (Fr. *vigne,* "vine") 1. Foliage ornament around a capital letter in a manuscript. 2. Similar ornament filling space in a manuscript or printed book. 3. Any design or illustration which fades into the surrounding space without a definite border.

Warm color: A color, which suggests KINAESTHETIC sensations of warmness, such as red or yellow. See also ADVANCING COLOR.

Wash: A HUE or TINT applied in a thick transparent layer.

Watercolor: Water-soluble PIGMENTS, combined with water-soluble gum as a BINDER, and water as a MEDIUM, used to make transparent paint. Non-transparent water-soluble paints (e.g. DISTEMPER, GOUACHE) are strictly speaking not watercolors.

Wood engraving: A technique developed from the WOODCUT by Thomas Bewick in England in the late 18th century. The PRINT is made from a hardwood block which is cut across (rather than along) the grain, highly polished and engraved with a BURIN and other tools of various sections (rather than a knife and gouges). Parts of the block could also be reduced to a slightly lower level so that they would take less ink and also less pressure when printed. All these developments combined to produce effects of great subtlety. In color printing, a different block is used for each color and successive IMPRESSIONS made to create a full color image. Synonym: xylography. See also WHITE LINE ENGRAVING.

Major U.S. Art Galleries and Museums

This is a listing of the "major" galleries and museums in the United States. It includes addresses, phone numbers, and emails and web sites if available. In addition, of course, there are countless other great experiences in most cities. If a major gallery in your city doesn't exhibit any of these artists, don't let that keep you from visiting. When you do, just apply my tips, questions and filters to what they are exhibiting and be sure to ask the on-site staff where you might find these artists' work in your city (listed alphabetically by state/city).

ALABAMA

BIRMINGHAM MUSEUM OF ART

2000 Eighth Ave. North
Birmingham, AL 35203
205-254-2566
www.artsbma.org

MONTGOMERY MUSEUM OF FINE ARTS

P.O. Box 230819
Montgomery, AL 36123
334-244-5700
www.fineartsmuseum.com

MOBILE MUSEUM OF ART

4850 Museum Drive
P.O. Box 8426
Langan Park
Mobile, AL 36689
251-208-5200
www.mobilemuseumofart.com

HUNTSVILLE MUSEUM OF ART

300 Church Street
Huntsville, AL 35801
256-535-4350
www.hsvmuseum.org

ALASKA

ANCHORAGE MUSEUM OF HISTORY AND ARTS

121 W. Seventh Aveune
Anchorage, AK 99501
907-343-6173
www.ci.anchoragemuseum.org

ARIZONA

PHOENIX ART MUSEUM

1625 North Central Ave
Phoenix, AZ 85004
602-257-1222
www.phxart.org

UNIVERSITY ART MUSEUM

Arizona State University Art Museum

Nelson Fine Arts Center and Matthews Center

Arizona State University
Tempe, AZ 85287
480-965-2787

TUCSON MUSEUM OF ART

140 N. Main Avenue
Tucson, AZ 85701
520-624-2333
www.tucsonarts.com

ARKANSAS

ARKANSAS ART CENTER

9th & Commerce/Macarthur Park
P.O. Box 2137
Little Rock, AK 72203-2137
501-373-4000
www.arkarts.com

CALIFORNIA

GALLERY C

1225 Hermosa Ave.
Hermosa Beach, CA 90254
310-798-0102
www.galleryc.com

THE FINE ARTS MUSEUMS OF SAN FRANCISCO
CALIFORNIA PALACE OF THE LEGION OF HONOR

100 34th Ave.
San Francisco, CA 94121
415-863-3330
www.thinker.org

PASADENA MUSEUM OF CALIFORNIA ART

490 E. Union St.
Pasadena, CA, 91101
(626) 568-3665
www. pmcaonline.org

M.H. DEYOUNG MUSEUM

75 Tea Garden Dr.
Golden Gate Park
San Francisco, CA 94118
415-750-3600

HUNTINGTON LIBRARY ART COLLECTIONS AND BOTANICAL GARDEN

1151 Oxford Rd.
San Marino, CA 91108
626-405-2100
www.huntington.org

FRESNO METROPOLITAN MUSEUM

1515 Van Ness Avenue
Fresno, CA 93721
559-441-1444
www.fresnomet.org

THE IRVINE MUSEUM

18881 Von Karman, Ste. 100
Irvine, CA 92612
949-476-2565
www.irvinemuseum.org

LAGUNA ART MUSEUM
307 Cliff Drive
Laguna Beach, CA 92651
949-494-8971
www.lagunaartmuseum.org

LONG BEACH MUSEUM OF ART
2300 E. Ocean Blvd.
Long Beach, CA 90803
562-439-2119
www.lbma.org

ORANGE COUNTY MUSEUM OF ART
850 San Clemente Drive
Newport Beach, CA 92660
949-759-1122
www.ocma.net

NORTON SIMON MUSEUM
411 W. Colorado Blvd.
Pasadena, CA 91105
626-449-6840
www.nortonsimon.org

LOS ANGELES COUNTY MUSEUM OF ART
5905 Wilshire Blvd
Los Angeles, CA 90036
323-857-6000
www.lacma.org

J. PAUL GETTY MUSEUM
1200 Getty Center Drive
Los Angeles, CA 90049
310-440-7300
www.getty.edu

CROCKER ART MUSEUM
216 O Street
Sacramento, CA 95814
916-264-5423
www.crockerartmuseum.org

THE BOWERS MUSEUM
2002 North Main Street
Santa Ana, CA 92706
714-567-3680
www.bowers.org

MUSEUM OF CONTEMPORARY ART/SAN DIEGO
700 Prospect Street
La Jolla, CA 92037
858-454-3541
www.mcasandiego.org

SAN DIEGO MUSEUM OF ART
1450 El Prado
Balboa Park, San Diego, CA
619-232-7931
www.sdmart.com

SAN FRANCISCO ART INSTITUTE

800 Chestnut Street
San Francisco, CA 94133
415-771-7020
www.sanfranciscoart.edu

SAN JOSE MUSEUM OF ART

110 S. Market Street
San Jose, CA 95113
408-271-6840
www.sjmusart.org

SANTA BARBARA MUSEUM OF ART

1130 State Street
Santa Barbara, CA 93101
805-963-4364
www.sbmuseart.org

COLORADO

THE DENVER ART MUSEUM

100 W. 14th Ave. Pkwy.
Denver, CO 80204
720-865-5000
www.denverartmuseum.org

ASPEN ART MUSEUM

590 N. Mill Street
Aspen, CO 81611
970-925-8050
www.aspenartmuseum.org

BOULDER MUSEUM OF CONTEMPORARY ART

1750 13th Street
Boulder, CO 80302
303-443-2122
www.bmoca.org

CONNECTICUT

WADSWORTH ATHENEUM MUSEUM OF ART

600 Main Street
Hartford, CT 06103
860-278-2670
www.wadsworthatheneum.org

THE WILLIAM BENTON MUSEUM OF ART

245 Glenbrook Rd, U-140
University of Connecticut
Storrs, CT 06269
860-486-4520
www.benton.uconn.edu

DELAWARE

DELAWARE ART MUSEUM

2301 Kentmere Parkway
Wilmington, DE 19806
302-571-9590
www.delart.org

WINTERTHUR MUSEUM AND GALLERY

Rt. 52
Winterthur, DE 19735
800-448-3883
www.winterthur.org

FLORIDA

BOCA RATON MUSEUM OF ART

501 Plaza Real
Boca Raton, FL 33432
561-392-2500
www.bocamuseum.org

MUSEUM OF CONTEMPORARY ART

770 N. 125th Street
North Miami, FL 33161
305-893-6211
www.mocanomi.org

NORTON MUSEUM OF ART

1451 S. Olive Ave
West Palm Beach, FL 33401
561-832-5196
www.norton.org

ORLANDO MUSEUM OF ART

2416 N. Mills Ave
Orlando, FL 32803
407-896-4231
www.omart.org

THE MUSEUM OF FINE ARTS

255 Beach Drive N.E.
St. Petersburg, FL 33701
727-896-2667
www.fine-arts.org

GEORGIA

HIGH MUSEUM OF ART

1280 Peachtree Street
NE, Atlanta, GA 30309
404-733-HIGH
www.high.org

MORRIS MUSEUM OF ART

1 Tenth Street
Augusta, GA 30901
706-724-7501
www.themorris.org

HAWAII

THE CONTEMPORARY MUSEUM

2411 Makiki Height Drive
Honolulu, HI 96822
808-526-0232
www.tcmhi.org

IDAHO

BOISE ART MUSEUM

670 Julia Davis Drive
Boise, ID 83702
208-345-8330
www.boiseartmuseum.org

ILLINOIS

THE ART INSTITUTE OF CHICAGO

111 South Michigan Avenue
Chicago, IL 60603
312-443-3600
www.artic.edu

MUSEUM OF CONTEMPORARY ART

220 E. Chicago Avenue
Chicago, IL 60611
312-280-2660
www.mcachicago.org

INDIANA

INDIANAPOLIS MUSEUM OF ART

400 Michigan Rd.
Indianapolis, IN 46208
317-920-2660
www.ima-art.org

SNITE MUSEUM OF ART

University of Notre Dame
Notre Dame, IN 46556
574-631-7960
www.nd.edu/~sniteart/

IOWA

CEDAR RAPIDS MUSEUM OF ART

410 Third Ave. SE
Cedar Rapids, IA 52401
319-366-7503
www.crma.org

DES MOINES ART CENTER

4700 Grand Avenue
Des Moines, IA 50312
515-277-4405
www.desmoinesartcenter.org

SIOUX CITY ART CENTER

225 Nebraska Street
Sioux City, IA 51101
712-279-6272
www.siouxcityartcenter.org

UNIVERSITY OF IOWA MUSEUM OF ART

150 North Riverside Drive
Iowa City, IA 52242
319-335-1727
www.uiowa.edu/uima

KANSAS

MULVANE ART MUSEUM

1700 SW College
Topeka, KA 66621
785-231-1010
www.washburn.edu

WICHITA ART MUSEUM

619 Stackman Drive
Wichita, KA 67203
316-268-4921
www.wichitaartmuseum.org

KENTUCKY

THE SPEED MUSEUM

2035 South Third Street
Louisville, KY 40208
502-634-2700
www.speedmuseum.org

UNIVERSITY OF KENTUCKY ART MUSEUM

Rose Street and Euclid Avenue
Lexington, KY 40506
859-257-5716
www.uky.edu

LOUISIANA

ALEXANDRIA MUSEUM OF ART

P.O. Box 1028
Alexandria, LA 71303
318-443-3458
www.themuseum.org

NEW ORLEANS MUSEUM OF ART

P.O. Box 19123
New Orleans, LA 70179
504-488-2631
www.noma.org

RW NORTON ART GALLERY

4747 Creswell Avenue
Shreveport, LA 71106
318-865-4201
www.softdisk.com/comp/norton

MAINE

THE FARNSWORTH ART MUSEUM

356 Main Street
Rockland, Maine 04841
207-596-6457
www.farnsworthmuseum.org

PORTLAND MUSEUM OF ART
Seven Congress Square
Portland, Maine 04101
207-775-6148
www.portlandmuseum.org

MARYLAND

BALTIMORE MUSEUM OF ART
Art Museum Drive
Baltimore, MD 21218
410-396-7100
www.artbma.org

WASHINGTON COUNTY MUSEUM OF FINE ARTS
P.O. Box 423
Hagerstown, Maryland 21741
301-739-5727
www.washcomuseum.org

MASSACHUSETTS

MUSEUM OF FINE ARTS
Avenue of the Arts
465 Huntington Avenue
Boston, MA 02115
617-267-9300
www.mfa.org

THE INSTITUTE OF CONTEMPORARY ART
955 Boylston Street
Boston, MA 02115
617-266-5152
www.icaboston.org

WORCESTER ART MUSEUM

55 Salisbury Street
Worcester, MA
508-799-4406
www.worcesterart.org

MICHIGAN

DETROIT INSTITUE OF ARTS

5200 Woodward Avenue
Detroit, MI 48202
313-833-7900
www.dia.org

FLINT INSTITUTE OF ARTS

1120 E. Kearsley Street
Flint, MI 48503
810-234-1695
www.flintarts.org

GRAND RAPIDS ART MUSEUM

155 Division North
Grand Rapids, MI 49503
616-831-1000
www.gramonline.org

KALAMAZOO INSTITUTE OF ARTS MUSEUM

314 South Park Street
Kalamazoo, MI 49007
269-349-7775
www.kiarts.org

MINNESOTA

CRANEBROOK ART MUSEUM

39221 Woodward Ave.
Bloomfield Hills, MN 48303
248-645-3300

MUSKEGON MUSEUM OF ART

296 W. Webster Ave.
Muskegon, MN 49440
231-720-2570
www.muskegonartmuseum.org

THE MINNEAPOLIS INSTITUTE OF ARTS

2400 Third Avenue South
Minneapolis, MN 55404
612-870-3131
www.artsmia.org

WALKER ART CENTER

Vineland Place
Minneapolis, MN
612-375-7622
www.walkerart.org

MISSISSIPPI

MISSISSIPPI MUSEUM OF ART

201 E. Pascagoula Street
Jackson, MS 39201
601-960-1515
www.msmuseumart.org

LAUREN ROGERS MUSEUM

565 N. Fifth Avenue
Laurel, MS 39441
601-649-6374
www.lrma.org

MISSOURI

SAINT LOUIS ART MUSEUM

1 Fine Arts Drive
St. Louis, MO 63110
314-721-0072
www.slam.org

KEMPER MUSEUM OF CONTEMPORARY ART

4420 Warwick Blvd.
Kansas City, MO 64111
816-753-5784
www.kemperart.org

MONTANA

MUSEUM OF THE ROCKIES

Montana State University
600 West Kagy Blvd.
Bozeman, MT 59717
406-994-2251
www.montana.edu/wwwmor

MONTANA MUSEUM OF ART AND CULTURE AT THE UNIVERSITY OF MONTANA

Performing Arts and Radio/Television Center
Missoula, MT 59812
406-243-2019
www.umt.edu/partv/famus/default.htm

NEBRASKA

JOSLYN ART MUSEUM

2200 Dodge Street
Omaha, NE 68102
402-342-3300
www.joslyn.org

MUSEUM OF NEBRASKA ART

2401 Central Avenue
Kearney, NE 68847
308-865-8559
www.monet.unk.edu/mona

NEVADA

NEVADA MUSEUM OF ART

160 W. Liberty Street
Reno, NV 89501
775-329-3333
www.nevadaart.org

NEW HAMPSHIRE

THE CURRIER GALLERY OF ART

201 Myrtle Way
Manchester, NH 03104
603-669-6144
www.currier.org

HOOD MUSEUM OF ART

Wheelock Street, Dartmouth College
Hanover, NH 03755
603-646-2808
www.dartmouth.edu/~hood

NEW JERSEY

THE MONTCLAIR ART MUSEUM

3 South Mountain Ave
Montclair, NJ 07042
973-746-5555
www.montclair-art.com

THE NEWARK MUSEUM

49 Washington Street
P.O. Box 540
Newark, NJ 07101
973-596-6550
www.newarkmuseum.org

THE NOYES MUSEUM OF ART

Lily Lake Road
Oceanville, NJ 08231
609-652-8848
www.noyesmuseum.org

NEW MEXICO

MUSEUM OF NEW MEXICO

706 Camino Lejo 87504
Santa Fe, NM
505-476-1200
www.moifa.org

ROSWELL MUSEUM AND ART CENTER

100 W. Eleventh Street
Roswell, NM 88201
505-624-6744
www.roswellmuseum.org

NEW YORK

ALBRIGHT-KNOX ART GALLERY

1285 Elmwood Avenue
Buffalo, NY 14222
716-882-8700
www.albrightknox.org

BROOKLYN MUSEUM OF ART

200 Eastern Parkway
Brooklyn, NY 11238
718-638-5000
www.brooklynart.org

GUGGENHEIM MUSEUM

1071 Fifth Ave.
New York, NY 10128
212-423-3500
www.guggenheim.org

THE MUSEUM OF MODERN ART

11 W. 53rd Street
New York, NY 10019
212-708-9403
www.moma.org

THE METROPOLITAN MUSEUM OF ART

1000 Fifth Avenue at 82nd Street
New York, NY 10028
212-535-7710
www.metmuseum.org

NORTH CAROLINA

NORTH CAROLINA MUSEUM OF ART

2110 Blue Ridge road
Raleigh, NC 27699
919-839-6262
www.ncartmuseum.org

ASHVILLE ART MUSEUM

21 South Park Square
P.O. Box 1717
Asheville, NC 28802
828-253-3227
www.ashevilleart.org

WEATHERSPOON ART GALLERY

P.O. Box 26170
Greensboro, NC 27402
336-334-5770
www.uncg.edu/wag

NORTH DAKOTA

NORTH DAKOTA MUSEUM OF ART

P.O. Box 7305
Grand Forks, ND 58202
701 777-4195
www.ndmoa.com

OHIO

THE CLEVELAND MUSEUM OF ART

11150 E. Boulevard
Cleveland, OH 44106
216-421-7340
www.clemusart.com

THE CONTEMPORARY ARTS CENTER
115 E Fifth Street
Cincinnati, OH 45202
513-345-8400
www.spiral.org

WEXNER CENTER FOR THE ARTS
The Ohio State University
1871 North High Street
Columbus, OH 43210
614-292-3535
www.wexarts.org

OKLAHOMA

THE PHILBROOK MUSEUM OF ART
2727 South Rockford Rd.
Tulsa, OK 74114
918-748-5309 or 800-324-7941
www.philbrook.org

OREGON

CORVALLIS ART CENTER
700 SW Madison
Corvallis, OR 97333
541-754-1551
www.caclbca.org

PORTLAND ART MUSEUM
1219 S.W. Park Ave.
Portland, OR 97205
503-226-2811
www.pam.org

PENNSYLVANIA

INSTITUTE OF CONTEMPORARY ART

118 S. 36th Street
Philadelphia, PA 19104
215-898-7108
www.icaphila.org

PHILADELPHIA MUSEUM OF ART

Benjamin Franklin Parkway at 26th Street
Philadelphia, PA 19101
215-763-8100
www.philamuseum.org

JAMES A MICHENER ART MUSEUM

138 South Pine Street
Doylestown, PA 18901
215-340-9800
www.michenerartmuseum.org

WESTMORELAND MUSEUM OF AMERICAN ART

221 North Main Street
Greensburg, PA 15601
724-837-1500
www.wmuseumaa.org

TENNESSEE

HUNTER MUSEUM OF AMERICAN ART

10 Bluff View
Chattanooga, TN 37403
423-267-0968
www.huntermuseum.org

KNOXVILLE MUSEUM OF ART
1050 World's Fair Park
Knoxville, TN 37916
865-525-6101
www.knoxart.org

THE MEMPHIS BROOKS MUSEUM OF ART
1934 Poplar Avenue
Memphis, TN 38104
901-544-6200
www.brooksmuseum.org

TEXAS

DALLAS MUSEUM OF ART
1717 N. Harwood
Dallas, TX 75201
214-922-1200
www.dm-art.org

MODERN ART MUSEUM OF FORT WORTH
Cultural District
3200 Darnell Street
Fort Worth, TX 76107
817-738-9215
www.mamfw.org

THE MUSEUM OF FINE ARTS, HOUSTON
1001 Bissonnet
Houston, TX 77005
713-639-7300
www.mfah.org

CONTEMORARY ART MUSEUM
5216 Montrose Blvd.
Houston, TX 77006
713-284-8250
www.camh.org

SAN ANTONIO MUSEUM OF ART
200 West Jones Ave.
San Antonio, TX 78215
210-978-8100
www.sa-museum.org

UTAH

BRAITHWAITE FINE ARTS MUSEUM AND GALLERY
290 West Center Street
Cedar City, UT 84720
435-586-5432
www.suu.edu/pva/artgallery

UTAH MUSEUM OF FINE ARTS
410 Campus Center Drive
Salt Lake City, UT 84112
801-581-7332
www.umfa.utah.edu

SPRINGVILLE MUSEUM OF ART
126 E. 400 SOUTH
Springville, UT 84663
801-489-2727
www.shs.nebo.edu/museum/museum.html

VERMONT

THE BENNINGTON MUSEUM

West Main Street
Bennington, VT 05201
802-447-1571
www.benningtonmuseum.com

ROBERT FLEMING MUSEUM

61 Colchester Ave.
Burlington, VT 05405
802-656-0750
www.uvm.edu

VIRGINIA

VIRGINIA MUSEUM OF FINE ARTS

2800 Grove Ave.
Richmond, VA 23221
804-340-1400
www.vmfa.state.va.us

CHRYSLER MUSEUM OF ART

245 W. Olney Road
Norfolk, VA 23510
757-664-6200
www.chrysler.org

WEST VIRGINIA

THE HUNTINGTON MUSEUM OF ART

2033 McCoy Rd
Huntington, WV 25702
304-529-2701
www.hmoa.org

WASHINGTON

BELLEVUE ART MUSEUM

510 Bellevue Way NE
Bellevue, WA 98004
425-519-0770
www.bellevueart.org

FRYE ART MUSEUM

704 Terry Ave.
Seattle, WA 98104
206-622-9250
www.fryeart.org

SEATTLE ART MUSEUM

100 University Street
Seattle, WA 98101
206-654-3100
www.seattleartmuseum.org

WASHINGTON, DC/DISTRICT OF COLUMBIA

CORCORAN GALLERY OF ART

17th Street & New York Ave NW
Washington, DC 20006
202-639-1700
www.corcoran.org

SMITHSONIAN AMERICAN ART MUSEUM

750 Ninth Street, N.W.
Washington, DC 20001
202-275-1500
www.nmaa.si.edu

WISCONSIN

MADISON ART CENTER

211 State Street
Madison, WI 53703
608-257-0158
www.madisonartcenter.org

INSTITUTE OF VISUAL ARTS

3253 N. Downer Ave.
Milwaukee, WI 53211
414-229-5070
www.uwm.edu

MILWAUKEE ART MUSEUM

700 North Art Museum Drive
Milwaukee, WI 53202
414-224-3200
www.mam.org

THE SHEBOYGAN ART MUSEUM

123 Letsby Avenue
Sheboygan, WI 53801
920-976-1212
www.art-museum.org

WYOMING

THE UNIVERSITY OF WYOMING ART MUSEUM

2111 Willet Drive
Laramie, WY 82071
307-766-6622
www.uwyo.edu/artmuseu